The Power of Process

This book should be required reading for IT professionals who wish to enter into meaningful business conversations with their executives.
Andrew Spanyi, Author of *More for Less: The Power of Process Management*

This is an essential reference for directors and executives trying to navigate the alphabet soup of the BPM and SOA worlds. Kiran breaks technical topics down into plain, everyday language, which is essential to communicating effectively with a broad audience.
Scott Mark, Enterprise Architect,
Fortune 250 medical technology company

The book is thoroughly readable and enjoyable while being informative. I strongly recommend this book for business managers, business school professors, and their students.
Dr. Murali Mohan Narasipuram, Associate Professor,
City University of Hong Kong

A very compelling read that paints the picture of corporate waste due to a lack of end-to-end process and accountability. Kiran has done a superb job of making this a fascinating read.
Billa Bhandari, Founder & CEO, Akoura

This is an insightful and enjoyable book. Kiran Garimella demystifies business and technology jargon through an entertaining story. He takes current and complex issues in information technology and makes them very easy to understand.
Dr. Salman A. Mufti, Assistant Professor,
Queen's School of Business

The Power of Process

Unleashing the Source of Competitive Advantage

Kiran K. Garimella

Meghan-Kiffer Press
Innovation at the Intersection of Business and Technology
Tampa, Florida, USA
www.mkpress.com

This book is a work of fiction. Any references to historical events, real people, or real locales are used fictitiously. Other names, places, characters, and incidents are the product of the author's imagination, and any resemblance to actual events or locales or persons, living or dead, is entirely coincidental.

Publisher's Cataloging-in-Publication Data

Garimella, Kiran K.
The Power of Process: Unleashing the Source of Competitive Advantage/ Kiran K. Garimella, - 1st ed.
p. cm.
  Includes appendix.
  ISBN 10: 0-929652-06-1 ISBN 13: 978-0929652-06-1

  1. Management. 2. Leadership. 3. Technological innovation. 4. Executive ability. 5. Organizational Effectiveness. 6. Strategic planning. 7. Organizational change. 8. Re-engineering (Management) 9. Process control. I. Garimella, Kiran. II. Title

HD58.87.G6369 2006   2006930946
658.4'063–dc21   CIP

Cover Photo: National Weather Service / James Minot
Book's Web site: www.mkpress.com/power
Published by Meghan-Kiffer Press
310 East Fern Street — Suite G
Tampa, FL 33604 USA

Company and product names mentioned herein are the trademarks or registered trademarks of their respective owners.

Meghan-Kiffer books are available at special quantity discounts for corporate education and training use. For more information write Special Sales, Meghan-Kiffer Press, Suite G, 310 East Fern Street, Tampa, Florida 33604 or email admin at mkpress.com

---

Meghan-Kiffer Press
Innovation at the Intersection of Business and Technology
Tampa, Florida, USA
www.mkpress.com
Printed in the United States of America.   SAN 249-7980
MK Printing 10 9 8 7 6 5 4 3 2 1

Contents

Preface

Business Process Management (BPM for short) is an exciting discipline that offers a set of refreshing ideas to address the ubiquitous problem of business-IT alignment. Given the ever-expanding digitization of business activities and the ability of companies to distribute their operations worldwide, the bogey of the IT-business divide cannot be ignored any longer. Pretending that IT is nothing more than spreadsheets and word-processing, that it may be relegated to some monolithic back-office ERP, that it does not really matter, and refusing to invest any time in gaining an understanding of recent advances in the field, is tantamount to gross negligence.

While BPM is usually presented as a technical solution, I contend that it is not primarily a technology or a tool issue. BPM has far-reaching consequences for the organization, its culture, and competitiveness. This book is an exploration of how BPM helps in innovation, productivity, compliance, and controllership. In so doing, BPM facilitates a tight synchronization between IT and the business. The book examines and lays bare the various nuances of what such a tight coupling really means. The goal of the book is to build awareness of BPM.

While the core concepts of BPM are themselves not new, what is exciting about it is the way they can be—and to some extent are—packaged and enabled through recent advances in software development. The ever-expanding high-speed broadband networks, the maturation of standards, and the increasing acceptance of the Internet model also contribute to bringing BPM down from the ivory towers to the practitioners.

An overview of the book: The introductory chapter (the only non-fiction chapter in the book) sets the context for business process management, describes its relationship to systems theory, and provides a general background for the key themes.

Chapter 1, 'Who Moved My Life?' begins with a dialog that describes what is ostensibly the problem of inadequate return on investment from IT projects. However, the dialog motivates the discovery of a deeper problem: the inability of IT to contribute to a 'return on time.' A future chapter extends this indictment of IT to a lack of support for innovation, but identifies it as an issue that goes beyond just IT, and provides ideas on how to address it.

The challenge with presenting the subject of BPM, which has its roots in information technology, to a wider non-technical audience, is the prevalence of technical acronyms and jargon. Chapter 2 introduces the colorful management and technology guru, Dr. Jeffrey Sterllings, who, over the course of this chapter and the next, explains the fundamental concepts behind many of the popular TLAs[1] that support BPM.[2] These include, among others, SOA, XML, BPMN, BPEL, EAI, MDA, and BAM.[3] The goal in this chapter, and also throughout the book, is not to provide a technical dissertation on these acronyms, but to arm the reader with sufficient understanding of the core ideas so that the use of acronyms throughout the book will not be a distraction. The reader is not expected to have any background in IT, and should not expect to become an expert in these topics by reading this book. Additionally, the reader may refer to the glossary at the end for an expansion of the acronyms.

BPM facilitates an in-depth examination of a company's business processes. This begs the question, *why do we need to study business processes?* One obvious response is, *to improve them.* Six Sigma happens to be a well-tested methodology and framework for improving business processes and managing the consequent change. Professionals who are familiar with Six Sigma may like to know how BPM fits with Six Sigma. *Does BPM replace Six Sigma? Does one include the other? Do they compete or are they complementary?* Read chapter 4, 'Will BPM Deep Six Six Sigma?' to find out.

---

[1] TLA, which is itself a TLA, stands for *Three-Letter Acronym.* If you think that a four-letter acronym would be an FLA, you'd be vastly mistaken; in the best tradition of computer science nerdiness, a four-letter acronym is known as an ETLA, which stands for *Extended TLA.* ETLA, in a bizarre instance of recursion, is itself an ETLA.

[2] BPM: Business Process Management, the main subject of this book.

[3] Come on! Read the rest of the book!

An indicator of the level of sophistication and maturity of a technology is the ability of the technology to be self-aware. For example, an elevator system that includes monitors to detect excess weight, loose cables, and other failure points is superior to one that does not. Chapter 5, 'The Omniscient Process,' discusses what it means for business processes to be self-aware. Just as a critical mass of neurons is necessary to achieve biological self-awareness, BPM provides the critical functionality for self-description of processes.

While chapter 5 looks at the notion of self-awareness of processes from the perspective of knowledge management, chapter 6, 'A Process on the Freudian Couch,' covers the same from the perspective of processes that have to live and communicate with other processes. One personified process describes its anguish over its siloed isolation from other processes, while Dr. Sterllings, in the role of a psychiatrist, leads his 'patient' to discover the requirements for a happy life in process-world.

In chapter 7, Dr. Sterllings meets his old mentor to discuss the relationship between BPM, SOA, XML, and BAM. These are tied together into what may be loosely described as a 'life-cycle' of processes. While BPM generally provides the DNA and the chemicals to bring processes to life, SOA is the physio-skeletal system that allows the life-form to move about and function. XML may be likened to the nervous system that serves as the medium and protocol of communication. To stretch the analogy a bit further, just as RNA acts as a messenger and translator of the genetic code into proteins, MDA (Model-Driven Architecture) provides a technology-neutral way of translating the BPM architecture into practical designs. BAM provides the feedback loop, the pain-pleasure principle, and the deep control mechanism that keeps a life-form in homeostasis and agile in a constantly changing environment. An informal, tongue-in-cheek cybernetic equation ties these components together.

The next three chapters (8, 9, and 10) should especially be read in sequence; they cover the most important rationale for strategic IT spending—innovation and growth. Nicholas Carr's article and subsequent book, 'IT Doesn't Matter,' rankled many IT professionals and made their bosses wonder if they should be writing out pink slips. However, a large portion of IT spending goes to ensure the lights are kept on, while an equally large amount of money is poured down the drain on ill-conceived ERP and legacy migration projects. Companies that make a big deal about productivity and cost-out are those that most likely have nothing better to do, i.e., they have no strong pipeline of innovation and growth. The spirited dialog in these three chapters reflects the highly controversial nature of this topic.

An earlier chapter (chapter 4) described the connection between BPM and Six Sigma, establishing the motivation for process improvement. Companies that are deep into the Six Sigma methodology may wonder if such heavy statistical machinery is really required for all process improvement efforts. The Lean methodology suggests a less intensive alternative. Chapter 11 goes into some, but not exhaustive, detail about the Lean methodology; specifically, the discussion revolves around the interplay between BPM and Lean.

While the earlier chapters focused on the 'front-end' of BPM, namely, modeling, analysis, process improvement, and the justification for BPM (i.e., innovation and growth), the focus now shifts to the operational issues of BPM, namely, keeping processes in control, ensuring compliance, and the controllership of the business. Chapter 12 uses an episode of sailing to tease out the nature of controls and feedback loops to motivate concepts in Business Activity Monitoring.

Continuing on with the topic of controllership, chapter 13 begins with a situation that keeps many CEOs and CFOs awake at night.[4] The fictional company in the book finds, through an extensive Board-sanctioned internal audit, that it not only lacks good regulatory controls, but it also has shortcomings in its management controls. The subject of controllership and compliance is treated in a general way, not as a knee-jerk reaction to the latest regulatory threat. The concept of enterprise risk management—a comprehensive way to identify, monitor, and manage all varieties of risk—is

---

[4] The numbering of this ominous chapter is purely coincidental.

introduced. The protagonist explains how BPM, while not a silver-bullet, facilitates risk management.

How do BPM and SOA affect the daily activities of the IT and Quality department? What cultural changes follow as a consequence of adopting BPM? At a tactical level, how is the gap between IT and the business bridged? Possible answers to these questions form the focus of chapter 14, 'United We Stand.' Jeffrey Sterllings proposes the three laws of organizational synergy that are faintly reminiscent of Asimov's three laws of robotics.[5]

At this point in the book, the other characters in the story, and hopefully the reader, have acquired an appreciation for the power of business process management. In particular, they realize that BPM is not solely a technical topic, that its adoption has cultural and organizational ramifications. The final chapter (chapter 15), 'From SOA to POA, From CIO to CPO,' proposes ideas to move a company from a set of functional silos to a process-based dynamic organism that conducts its business through customer value chains. A similar morphing of the role of the Chief Information Officer into a Chief Process Officer is also described. Fully in keeping with the spirit of Asimov's own evolution of the three laws of robotics,[6] a zeroeth law of organizational synergy is introduced to round out the discussion.

How to read the book: The book does not have a strict plot in the sense of a murder mystery novel. It portrays a journey of awareness and discovery of BPM. The first chapter sets up the problem in an innocuous setting, and is essential to the rest of the book; later chapters introduce numerous other related issues and show how BPM attacks them. In addition to this first chapter, I strongly recommend that the next two chapters, which discuss the jargon of BPM and related fields, be read so that the acronyms do not hinder the reader. Chapters 8, 9, and 10 are also to be read sequentially.

---

[5] Isaac Asimov, 'Runaround,' a short story published in 1942. The three laws of robotics have appeared in many of his other subsequent works; they are also referenced in some textbooks on robotics.
[6] Asimov added a zeroeth law in his book, 'Robots and Empire,' 1985.

The very last chapter (chapter 15) brings together the various themes of the book and concludes with some follow-up ideas; obviously, it is beneficial to read this last. The other chapters are less dependent on each other (though there may be an occasional cross-reference). On the whole, it is perhaps best to read the book in sequence. Most importantly, I hope to entertain the reader with fictional dialog, limericks, aphorisms, and other devices. Unlike the regular textbooks and serious professional books, there are no pictures, charts, or tables (except for one in the very last chapter).

Since BPM has far-reaching implications, I've tried to present ideas that hopefully resonate with various categories of readers, such as theorists, purists, academics, practitioners, consultants, researchers, senior executives, junior professionals, and vendors. This is a very diverse audience, and I hope the reader will bear with me if I belabor a point for the benefit of some of the other readers.

In this age of information overload, it was an important goal for me to keep the busy reader's attention; my experimental hypothesis is that a short novel with small, quick-paced chapters should do the trick. Key points are summarized at the end of each chapter.

Target audience: Who will benefit from this book? While my publisher and I would love it if *everyone* on the planet bought and read the book, the people who would really benefit are in one or more of these categories:

- knowledge workers whose professional charter is to examine, manage, or improve processes (examples of such knowledge workers are business analysts, quality experts, and process analysts—people whose professional raison d'être is the constant examination, documentation, specification, analysis, and improvement of business processes);
- managers who are being (or will be) bombarded with the importunings of BPM vendors and consultants;
- managers whose professional job description calls for more than just the handling of day-to-day operations and transactions (specifically, a manager whose job calls for some thought leadership in improving the way their business operates);

- senior managers or C-level executives who constantly worry (or should worry) about making their business run smoother, faster, more efficiently, and more responsively;
- senior executives who worry (or should worry even more) about redeploying time and attention into innovation and growth;
- vendors who need to strategize on how to enhance their products, add true value, and present a compelling case to their customers (product vendors in BPM, SOA, EAI, Six Sigma, LEAN, document management, compliance solutions, knowledge management, and content management will benefit);
- consultants and vendors providing professional services in the above fields;
- industry analysts tracking pioneering ideas in the above fields;
- professionals at all levels in information technology;
- researchers in MIS, decision science, management science, and computer science who are seeking promising new areas;
- undergraduate and graduate students in computer science, business administration, Management Information Systems, marketing, decision-sciences, MBA, etc., who want to learn more than what the traditional curricula offer;[7]
- professors who are being pestered with pesky questions by the above students;
- parents of the above students who don't feel they know what career options are possible for their kids, and therefore cannot enter into any meaningful dialog with them;
- people who are none of the above but who, tired of slinging hash or folding clothes, would like to break into new careers;
- people who feel offended because their profession isn't covered by any of the above categories.

What this book is not: The book makes no pretense of exhaustively covering the subject of business process management. There is no discussion of tools, BPM suites, methodologies, or vendor offerings. There are no recommendations on which tools to buy,

---

[7] Hopefully, educational institutions will include BPM in their course work.

which consulting companies to engage, or what specific standards and methodologies to employ. This book is not for technologists who want to know how to buy, install, setup, and use BPM tools. There is no treatment of IT programming, or any in-depth coverage of Six Sigma and Lean.

What this book is: It is hoped that the book will bring an awareness of process management to business leaders and senior executives, help technologists and Quality professionals socialize BPM within their companies, and lead the change in organizational culture. The book also exposes to all management and IT professionals a tantalizing career path in process management. Technical topics, such as SOA, XML, EAI, MDA, web services, and others are treated in a way that is expected to be accessible to non-IT professionals and managers. I hope the technically inclined reader, who may encounter a redundancy of definitions or descriptions of technical jargon, or a simplistic treatment of some of the concepts, will bear with me; this is deliberate and designed to make the non-IT reader feel at ease. If the non-technical reader is lost in an occasional technical fine point, it should not detract from an understanding of the main themes.

Acknowledgments: When I was graduate student, I was extremely fortunate to have a very indulgent professor as my advisor, who let me follow my intellectual curiosity to my heart's content. He also challenged me mercilessly. A typical interaction between us would occur in this manner:

Me: "Hi Professor K! I was reading this research paper that mentioned Calculus of Variations. I thought it was a fascinating technique. Do you know anything about it?"

Prof. K: "Oh, yes. I wrote a paper on it in the year 19XX."

Me: "Oh!"

A few days later, I would burst into his office with excitement.

Me: "Prof. K! There is a way to model information content of systems using the concept of information entropy…"

Prof. K., gently interrupting me, "Yes, Claude Shannon

introduced that concept way back in 1948. I used it in a research paper of mine in 19YY."

I exit his office, thinking, *Is there anything this man doesn't know?*

A few weeks later, I march into his office, this time confident that Prof. K. would be ignorant of this gem of a technique derived from thermodynamics that I had come upon purely by accident. After all, come on! Prof. K. is an expert in artificial intelligence, optimization theory, and computer science. But *physics?*

Me: "Here is a pretty neat little technique called maximum entropy that we could use to select the optimal distribution..."

Prof. K., casually reminiscing, "Oh yes, Jaynes' technique of using maximum entropy to select the maximally informative probability distribution from a family of distributions...I gave a lecture about it in 19ZZ."

OK, point taken. I owe a great intellectual debt to Professor Gary Koehler, John B. Higdon Professor of Decision and Information Science, Warrington College of Business Administration, University of Florida. He inspired me to push myself to the frontiers of knowledge, and I spent five glorious years as a doctoral student pursuing them. Since then, he has unstintingly given his time and advice throughout the years. As if this were not enough, Prof. Koehler also extensively reviewed this manuscript over several drafts. He is a true guru!

Without practical grounding, the grandest theories flounder and get relegated to a footnote in history. I thank Steve McCrystal (ex-CIO, and at the time of this writing, Managing Director of Operations and Quality, GE Healthcare Financial Services) for his perspectives on overcoming the challenges of organizational culture and his practical advice on fostering change.

I wish to thank the following colleagues, ex-colleagues, friends, and professionals for sharing ideas through extended discussions and emails, reviewing the manuscript, and suggesting numerous improvements: Sanjeev Acharya, Calvin Barksdale, Raman (Ron) Batra, Christine Bohte, Justin Chiu, Geoff Elliott, James Gunn, Bengt Hagstrom, Saugata Halder, Chris Hodges, Rajeev Jain, Mike Kosiarek, Jodie Kotlarek, Cameron Kruger, Atul Kumar, Ravi

Madugula, Chris Middleton, Norton Paratela, Ganesh Parkar, Srinadh Palaparthi, Sinan Si Alhir, Samir Singh, Guy Tumbleson, Vivek Velso, Vivek Rao, Venkat Viswanathan, and Krishnan Vijayaraghavan. John Parodi, Jason Matthews, and Michael Guttman helped fill a gap by alerting me to the importance of MDA, besides providing exhaustive and thoughtful comments on the rest of the manuscript; John Parodi also improved one of my limericks!

I deeply appreciate the time and effort of all these reviewers. I feel the book is richer for their review, since they come from diverse backgrounds at all levels, both in IT and non-IT. Any errors, of course, are mine.

Two of the chapters originally appeared in www.bptrends.org (though not in the exact same form). I am thankful to Paul Harmon and Celia Wolf for their encouragement.

Food is used as literary foil in some of the chapters. For culinary inspiration, I give thanks to Irma Rombauer and Marion Rombauer Becker for their classic work, *The Joy of Cooking*, and to the *Larousse Gastronomique*, the French classic, for unabashedly presenting recipes guaranteed to drive dedicated dieters into despair.

Dr. Bob Norris has been a good friend and mentor over the years. He has always been there for me, especially during challenging times. For that, I am truly thankful.

I would not be what I am today without the deep love of learning inculcated in me by my late father, G.S. Murthy, and the discipline of hard work shown to me by example by my mother, Dr. G. Seeta.

My daughters, Lillian and Angela, cheered me on despite this not being a children's action adventure book. My wife, Raji, showered love and encouragement, despite this not being a romance novel. They make what I do worthwhile.

Finally, the constant encouragement from my friend and mentor, Peter Fingar, was instrumental in bringing this book to light. He is a visionary, noted author, and a highly regarded speaker, whose interests are varied and not limited to IT and management.

Cast of Characters

Dr. Jeffrey Sterllings:
The mildly eccentric IT and management guru, the main character of this book.

Consolidated Enterprises

Rex Skiller.....................................Chairman of the Board

Barry Attwater..President & CEO

Ami Taylor.................................Barry's executive assistant

Marty Montrose...CIO

Dan Manning...CFO

Chuck Myers............Head of Process Improvement and Quality

Carl Sanders.......................................Chief of Operations

Mark Andersen......................................VP of Marketing

Nathan Edwards.....................................Internal Auditor

Miscellaneous

James St. Royal...an MBA student

François..a graduate student

Prof. Alfred Feinstein.........a brilliant scientist and Jeffrey's mentor

Introduction

When Ludwig von Bertalanffy[8] first propounded systems thinking as a new way to make sense of our world, there were three general reactions. The first was, "Ho hum…yawn." The second was, "This is revolutionary! Tell me more!" The third was a cautious "Sounds interesting, but I need to know more." Systems thinking eventually withstood the test of time and became ingrained into everyday life. Today, we don't talk about a storm. The meteorologist on the TV predicts, "A storm system is approaching," conjuring up in the minds of the viewers a cohort of furious thunderheads militantly marching towards them. We don't have swamps anymore. We have an ecosystem instead. If you are tired of the system of mosquito bites on your anatomical system, you could entertain yourself by reading the educational material on the monetary system on the web site of the Federal Reserve System.

Processes, like systems, are not new. There have always been processes, and always will be. However, just like systems, processes only recently acquired a distinct persona and position in our cognitive arena as a way to make sense of our world. The notion of a system was an open recognition that seemingly unrelated entities and phenomena are somehow related. It was an explicit acknowledgment that trying to understand each entity in isolation led to a partial and ultimately flawed understanding of reality. However, the focus of systems thinking was on the static structure of relationships. The focus of process thinking is on the dynamic movement of entities, or on the dynamic unfolding of phenomena. A system is a concept of being; a process is a concept of becoming.

---

[8] von Bertalanffy published his influential book, 'General Systems Theory' in 1968; while not the only early thinker on the subject, he is considered one of the most influential in the modern era.

A process is not merely a haphazard assortment of changing entities, like an impressionist composition of Debussy;[9] rather, there is a structure to the dynamism, much like a Beethoven symphony. Indeed, the analogy to classical music is so compelling that the word 'orchestration' is frequently used by process management tool vendors to describe the ability of their tools to coordinate the execution of multiple business processes and their interactions with the underlying IT[10] systems. There is the notion of the sequential nature of activities, possibly intermixed with some parallel activities. There is the notion of entities acting synchronously, where one entity waits for another entity to accomplish something before itself starting a task. There is the notion of asynchronicity, where entities act in seeming independence, but coordinated and controlled by a higher-level process (a *conductor*, if you will). There is also the notion of flow, the movement of data, transactions, and people from one process step to another. Finally, a process contains a codification of decision-making rules that either direct the flow within the process, or affect the activities that occur within any process step.

The power and importance of processes first burst into the realm of popular imagination with the now seemingly infamous business process reengineering revolution spearheaded by Hammer and Champy[11] in 1993. If you ignore the rhetoric of reengineering and the polemics against it, the day-to-day work of analyzing and managing processes is an indispensable and ongoing activity. At any given moment of the working day, there is at least one brain in every company that wonders why a particular process is broken or why it can't be improved. The statement of the problem may not be the same, or its solution may not be efficient (indeed, no action may be taken), but the thought itself seems inevitable, given the

---

[9] This is not to denigrate Debussy's music; indeed, impressionist music is a fascinating departure from formal classical structures.

[10] Information Technology

[11] See their *Reengineering the Corporation: A Manifesto for Business Revolution*

universal human predilection for finding faults and trying to fix them.[12]

What has changed since the mid-90's? Why the sudden resurgence in business process management? Is it just old wine in new bottles, or is this a completely new brand, like California champagne? Is it the next fad, the next excuse to layoff people, or are we on to something? Is it a new technology or a management theory?

I'll argue that business process management is a bit of all of the above. This is inevitable. By its very nature, process management cannot be new, but its elevation to an explicit domain of study is. It cannot be a fad, since problems with processes have existed ever since two ancient nomads in the hoary past got together to solve a territorial dispute.[13] The subject is riddled with some hype, as every vendor and management guru suddenly discovers that their product or theory has been about process management all along. Some irresponsible managers will adopt the hype to downsize their organizations into oblivion (if it is not business process management, they will find some other excuse).

However, as the thinking and understanding mature in this space, we may conclude that process management is here to stay. Process management is not solely information technology, despite the assurances of some vendors. It also includes the theory and best practices for managing organizational culture. The good news is that process management is a discipline whose time has come for very good reasons. The bad news is that there is no common understanding of what it is and how to take advantage of it.

Process management is not about downsizing; it is not about Six Sigma; it is not about buying an IT application. How does one get a handle on this subject? In this book, I have taken a non-traditional approach by presenting the material in a fictional format that is

---

[12] Systems theory, not to be outdone, bounced right back by influencing the development of *Business Process Management Systems*, as you'll see later in the book.

[13] The process they followed to solve their problem most likely involved plenty of blood and gore.

hopefully motivating and entertaining enough to read through completely.

The book has several key themes. First, business process management is like the proverbial elephant under scrutiny by four visually-challenged people; it can mean different things to different people because each person can see only one aspect of it. Second, business process management is less about technology and more about a mind-set. Third, paradoxically, business process management can be made a reality–and not just a highbrow management theory–by the latest advances in information technology.

The idea of BPM is deceptively simple, after you get through the clutter of acronyms. Because of this simplicity, it is easy to miss the true richness and versatility of process management. BPM is not a narrow (yet important) technical issue such as enterprise application integration. It is not a finite set of statistical techniques such as Six Sigma. It is not merely a highly generalized theory of management. It is at once a set of tools, a methodology, a cultural mindset, a set of pragmatic best practices, and an integrator par excellence of complementary ideas.[14] In this book, the fictional characters examine the fundamental ideas from various angles. Sometimes, it seems as if a concept is being treated redundantly. However, that concept is approached from a different context each time. At one time it may appear in a discussion on growth and innovation. At another time, it may surface in a dialog on productivity. Finally, the same concept may be revisited yet again in the context of compliance and controllership.

At the very outset, let me disabuse the reader of the notion that process management is a brand new fad, a hot-air management theory with no practical or theoretical substance to it. Process management has a rich history spanning three decades, with some serious academic work in process control, statistical control, pi calculus, Petri nets, concurrent systems, process modeling, information

---

[14] BPM is a new paradigm in management and information technology, but this word, *paradigm*, is guaranteed to cure insomnia, so I desist in using it except this one time.

architecture, analysis, design, workflows, patterns, and a myriad of other arcane topics. On the practical side, over one hundred fifty vendors compete aggressively in this space trying to define and distinguish themselves from their competition. More than two dozen technology and management analysts actively write in this space. Several key conferences have emerged in process management, and attendance at these events is surprisingly strong. Finally, there are thought-provoking authors and consultants who have an incredible diversity of experience in helping companies implement process management. Of course, none of this by itself guarantees sustained success, or even, in fact, the relevance or applicability of the discipline, but it does demonstrate the seriousness and intensity of purpose. I am confident that process management is massing up to be the next whirlwind of far-reaching, impactful ideas.

The reader can have three reactions to all this buzz about process management. On the one hand is the classic "Ho hum...yawn!" Such readers are in the danger of not benefiting from the enormous amount of real work that has been done on this subject for several years. On the other hand, the reaction may be "Fantastic! Where can I get it? Bring it on!" If so, such a reader is in the danger of being lead astray by the utopian blandishments of vendors. Gullibility is as bad as skepticism. Finally, the reaction may be a cautious enthusiasm, a willingness to keep an open mind, and to experiment in a small way before opening the floodgates to full acceptance. This last is the right attitude to bring to the BPM party.

Key Points

- Process thinking is a powerful way to focus on business processes, in contrast with systems thinking, which emphasizes the structure of, and relationship between, various entities.
- Process management took on new life due to breakthroughs in standards, innovation in new technologies, and cooperation between technologists.
- Process management is not merely new technology. It impacts the organization at many levels and integrates various perspectives into a coherent whole.

1 Who Moved My Life?

Barry Attwater, CEO of Consolidated Enterprises, emerged from his office and stepped over to his secretary's cubicle. Ami Taylor, phone cradled with casual skill between her head and shoulder, was in an earnest conversation with a friend. Her mouth was a pretty moue, blowing on her nails, arm held straight out. Seeing Barry, she whispered hastily into her phone, "I've got to go. I'll call you later. Bye!"

"Yes, boss?" she said, turning to Barry with a bright smile.

Her boss winced. "How many times have I told you not to call me *boss*? Especially not with that New York accent. Makes me feel like a Mafia don. Can you get Marty for me, please?"

Ami rapidly punched a few keys on her computer. "He's in a meeting with his IT[15] staff right now. He'll be done soon. His calendar is open after that."

"Snag him soon after his meeting and ask him to stop by. And oh, tell him to get the latest IT budget numbers, okay?"

"You got it, boss."

Barry threw up his hands in mock despair, and went back into his sanctum, shaking his head. *Some things are just meant to be*, he told himself. *Ami's incorrigible linguistic mannerisms, for one.*

He reached for the IT budget numbers. He shook his head some more. The trend did not make sense. He seemed to be spending more every year, and getting less and less for it. He pored over the detailed project financials. He carefully read the project notes, the explanations of variances to plan, and the options to get things back on track.

He was engrossed in this task for about twenty minutes, when there was a knock on the door. Marty Montrose, the Chief Information Officer, walked in. He had a file folder in his hand.

"You wanted to see me, boss?"

---

[15] Information Technology

Barry sighed deeply. The disease was spreading.

"Let's nip this thing in the bud. Stop calling me *boss*, and I'll promise not to throw you into the harbor with cement boots to keep your feet company."

Marty grinned. "Sorry! I caught it from you know who."

"Never mind all that. Did you bring your latest IT budget? Any changes from the last version you sent me?"

"Let's see. I did not send it to you directly. Finance messed around with it first."

Marty peered at the final number on Barry's copy.

"I knew it," he said. "Looks like the finance guys once more exercised their fiction-writing talents. They have trimmed my budget by over eight hundred thou."

"I can't say I entirely disagree with them. I've been looking at the numbers from the past few years. How come the growth rate of the IT budget is greater than the CAGR[16] of our business? It should be the other way around, don't you think?"

"Normally, I'd agree. But you must realize we stayed flat for the past three years. Now we have to catch up. The business is expanding pretty fast. Look at all the acquisitions we have made."

"But IT isn't really delivering more, is it? The number of projects have remained constant. The enhancements to our legacy systems have in fact decreased. I've read your notes and explanations. But I'd like you to restate in very simple words where you see the challenges."

"Very simply, the issue is this: we have a lot of overhead due to complexity. With each new application we build, we have to make sure it talks to the rest of the applications. We need to make sure that the integrity of information does not break down."

"I remember you telling me last year that we have to invest in an EAI[17] platform, whatever that means. Your team treated me to a dog-and-pony show about the exponential complexity of point-to-point communications, and how using an enterprising bus would

---

[16] Compound Annual Growth Rate
[17] Enterprise Application Integration

make the journey easier. What happened to all that?"

"I'm impressed you remember it! Only, we talked about using the Enterprise Bus."

Barry looked around uneasily. "We didn't go buy a corporate vehicle, did we?"

Marty laughed. "Come on Barry! Don't give me the Dilbert impression. We did install an EAI platform. The problem we have is that our biggest time consumption is in the upfront gathering of requirements."

Barry interrupted. "Looks like I was on the right track. Here," he said, pointing to a line graph. "I had Ami prepare a chart that shows the IT development cycle. On one axis we have the various project phases, plotted against elapsed time on the other axis. See how the requirements phase is out of balance when compared with the other phases? Here is that same graph, but now Ami added a trend line. It looks as if over the past three years, the proportion of time spent on requirements gathering kept going up. Either we are getting very detailed in our specifications, or we are getting inefficient. The only other possibility is that Ami made some horrible mistake."

Marty settled into a chair across from Barry.

"Ami did not make a mistake," he said. "You are right. I have been so down in the weeds that I did not notice that trend until last week. In fact, I just got out of a meeting that I had called to brainstorm the root causes of this very issue."

"And what did you find out? Or is that question premature?"

"I've some ideas. But first, I'd like to point out that if you had looked at similar graphs two years ago, you'd have seen that the development times were getting longer with each passing year, in addition to the increase in the requirements-gathering phase. Now look at the current graphs for the last three years. You'll see that the time for development has stabilized somewhat."

Barry peered at the graphs, his brow furrowed in concentration. "Hmm...you are right." He leaned back and laced his fingers behind his head. "So, how do you interpret that?"

Marty, who had attended a management training course in

communication a month ago, likewise leaned back and laced his fingers behind his head.

"The way I see it, our EAI platform has improved our development time line. After we got over the initial learning curve of six months, what we promised you in that dog-and-pony show started to yield fruit."

Barry nodded thoughtfully. "Okay, I get that. Makes sense. So what happened to the requirements part of the process?"

"My team gave me an earful just now about the inefficiencies in requirements-gathering. I think there are two fundamental causes for the horrendously long time we spend on getting requirements. One, our business analysts don't seem to have the right skill sets when it comes to documenting requirements and analyzing them."

"I thought that all they had to do was listen carefully, transcribe what they hear onto paper, and act as proxies for the business users. Even the spell-check is done by Microsoft Word. What other skill sets do they need?"

"They think their job is exactly as you described it. Therein lies the problem. They need to do more. They must ask the right questions, they must challenge assumptions, they must know how to model processes, they must know how to model data, and they must understand the capabilities of the IT systems as thoroughly as possible."

"In other words, they must be true analysts and not glorified scribes."

"Precisely."

"So, what's stopping them?"

"Expectations and training. I have to upscale their intellectual abilities. Also, they keep running into the second root cause."

"Ah, I was wondering about that."

"Chuck's PIQ[18] team is that other root cause. His function owns some of that process mapping, requirements gathering, and designing of improvements. My business analysts have conceded that ground to Chuck's team, so now they feel disenfranchised."

---

[18] Process Improvement and Quality

"Does it really matter who gathers the requirements? After all, it's one company and one team. Don't tell me a turf battle is shaping up."

"I don't think so. I'd nip that in the bud. I did emphasize the same thing to my team. The problem is that Chuck's team is not expected to be systems savvy. Their goal is very straight-forward: to apply Six Sigma methodology to come up with process improvements. They are ill-equipped to carry through their recommendations into technical designs. They don't see the problems on the maintenance side of IT."

"Let me see if I understand this. Your business analysts don't feel they own processes, so they have no incentive to understand the business in any detailed way. Chuck's black belts feel that they are only supposed to re-engineer business processes, but the improved designs are not at a level that is useful to IT. Your technical folks are fine qua technology, but they can't do a thing with the requirements they are getting because the requirements are either unclear, incorrect, or both."

"Not to mention that the requirements are subject to frequent change. Most meetings I have been in are very inefficient because everyone is asking each other, *How does that process work again? I thought it did this, but you are saying it does that?*"

"That happens in most meetings. That is why we have meetings. At the end of the meeting, they should be able to answer all those questions, or at least have a plan to get the answers."

"Maybe. But the funny thing about it is that six months later the same parties are back at the same table, discussing the same project, and they are still asking, *How does that work again? I thought it did this, but you are saying it does that?*"

"So our knowledge management is hopeless."

"We have no knowledge management to speak of. Our process for gathering knowledge is chaotic. On those rare occasions when we do have a good artifact of corporate knowledge, we have no controllership around it. It gets obsolete a week after it is compiled."

"What should be the ideal amount of time to spend on the upfront phases?"

"If you mean the discovery, definition, and analysis phases, loosely grouped together as the requirements-gathering phase, then I'd be happy if that upfront phase takes up no more and no less than forty percent of the total SDLC."

"Eh?"

"Sorry. Systems Development Life Cycle."

"I know why it takes you IT guys so long to understand each other. You use acronyms all over the place."

"So do you," retorted Marty. "What about ROI, ROE, ROA, AAGR, CAGR, CM, FASB, GAAP, MACRS, SOX, SHOES, and so on?"[19]

"There is no acronym called *SHOES*," laughed Barry. "But you have a point. Now let's look at our numbers here."

They leaned forward and huddled over the project timelines.

"It seems like we are spending a lot more than forty percent of our time on requirements," observed Barry, pointing to a few incriminating statistics.

"Well, forty percent is not an exact number, but a rough estimate," said Marty. "Other IT professionals may give you a slightly different number, but that's the number I feel comfortable with." He pointed to one of the projects. "But you are right. See, we spent over eight months trying to nail the requirements on this one. The actual coding was done in a month. We tested and fixed the bugs in fifteen days. That system has been working fine since deployment."

"Let's be careful here," cautioned Barry. "You are looking at elapsed time, not the actual effort. Do you have any way of capturing true effort."

"Yes, but sometimes the effort to track time is not worth it. I'd rather not create a regimented team. Our time would be better spent investing in think time, not clock-punch time. On this particular project, it would not have mattered anyway. We had a long elapsed time because twice in a row the critical subject matter experts on the project left the company. Our team had to go back

---

[19] See Glossary

each time to re-capture requirements."

"Our old friend, Knowledge Management, was missing?"

"In a way. Part of the credit for the delay must go to the learning curve the new employees had to go through to understand their function."

"It all boils down to having an efficient way to document business processes and use them in training."

"I couldn't agree more."

Barry got up and began to pace around the office impatiently.

"I can't put my finger on it, but another thing is troubling me. Maybe just talking about it will help."

He stopped and looked up at the ceiling for inspiration.

"My partners and I worked very hard to build this company, but boy, it was fun! Now I find that I'm dealing with crappy stuff all the time. Even though I'm working as hard as the time when I started the company, the return on my time–ROT, if you like–is getting smaller."

He turned and stabbed out an abrupt forefinger at Marty. "In fact, *you* should not be dealing with this crap all the time either. You and the rest of my direct team should be here with me, discussing strategy, business philosophy, best practices, new processes, innovation, and other fun stuff. I know we can't get away from day-to-day operations, but that shouldn't occupy all of our time."

It was Marty's turn to get up and start pacing. "I like your ROT concept. I never thought about it like that. I always liked working for you and this company, Barry. However, my job's become rather humdrum. The question is, how do we change the ho-hum-yawn to YO-HO-ROAR?"

"If you tell me, we'll both know," said Barry, drily. "Let's tackle the issue of time for a minute, no irony intended. How much fat would you estimate is present in those initial phases of a project?"

"You mean, if we had an ideal platform and process to manage our knowledge so we don't have to wander around in a fog all the time?

"Yes."

"I'd say we could get close to the forty percent proportion; of that, we could eliminate the absolute time of the phase by half."

"Let's see if I got this. We spend about forty percent of the total project time on discovery, definition, and analysis. Of that, about fifty percent is avoidable fat if only…yes? So, if we do the math, we could take on a whole lot more projects, right?"

"*If* we have the ideal 'system,' whatever that may be. Either we could do more projects, or implement improvements faster."

Barry looked at him thoughtfully for a long time. "It's my turn to bandy about some three-letter acronyms," he said, coming out of what seemed to be a communion with himself. "I refer to SOA and BPM.[20] I'll throw in *agility* for good measure, though that's not an acronym."

"What about them?" asked Marty, cautiously.

"I heard this guy speak at a CEO retreat. He went on and on about how BPM and SOA were the best things since chewing gum. I wasn't paying much attention because my mind was on that sticky regulatory issue concerning that acquisition we were going after, if you remember. But I noticed the speaker created a lot of fizz and bubble. I forgot his name, but it reminds me of sterling silver, maybe because he was bright and bubbly."

"Sterllings. Jeffrey Sterllings. He spoke at a BPM conference I happened to attend a few months ago. I spoke to him for a few minutes after his lecture. Very impressive."

"That's the guy! The funny thing is that since listening to him, my brain got attuned to those acronyms. I began to notice them more and more in a lot of the stuff I read. It seems like every other article and nearly every email from vendors is loaded with them."

"I know what you mean. It was only after my kids were born that I began to notice diaper boxes and strollers everywhere I went."

"I think you should give this guy a call. He gave me the impression that he had it all tied up into a neat package. I'd like to know if that package is for sale and if it is worth anything."

---

[20] Service-Oriented Architecture and Business Process Management. These are addressed in detail in subsequent chapters.

"If I remember," said Marty, rolling up his eyes in reminiscence, "his big takeaway at the conference was, start with process management, then implement using SOA, and you'll realize the benefits of agility. In time—my turn to say no irony intended—you'll get your time back which you can then redeploy into innovation and growth."

"Sounds neat, if you can pull it off. What I want to know is whether there's anything real to it, or is it just a lot of hot air?"

"I'll give him a jingle and start a conversation with him. Who knows, even if it is hot air, it may lift up this corporate balloon."

Key Points

- Enterprise integration technologies help simplify the exponential complexity of IT systems.
- Automation alone cannot remove inefficiencies in business processes; it is not a substitute for thinking, and cannot hide a dysfunctional corporate culture.
- Companies waste a lot more time in the non-technology phases of an IT project than they realize.
- The lack of sophisticated skills and tools for business analysts contributes to an inefficient requirements-gathering process.
- Quality and IT teams may get polarized by focusing on a limited aspect of processes.
- Inefficient and unsustainable process improvement efforts are caused by a lack of sophisticated techniques to manage processes.
- All these inefficiencies and a dysfunctional corporate culture erode the return on time. This in turn diverts management attention from the true goal of the company—innovation and growth.

2 TLAs, ETLAs, and Other Strange Beasts

Jeffrey Sterllings was comfortably ensconced in his home office, busily writing his new book, 'Pies in My Net: the Theoretical Foundations of Process Management,"[21] and was just completing page one hundred forty six. A smoldering pipe rested on its stand on the desk. A Waterford crystal snifter sat patiently to one side, replete with an ounce of Smirnoff, effervescing with club soda. The ice cubes in the glass fractured the frosty evening sunlight into a fractal scintillation. A geisha doll, exquisite in its alabaster mask, the colors harmonizing with the bright extravagance that is possible only to the Japanese, looked on in frozen amusement.

Jeff was on a roll, immersed in *schreibvergnugen*, the words flowing smoothly from neuron to electron, his fingers beating a musical tappity-tap on his laptop with the effortless digital athleticism of a concert pianist, when the phone rang. He glanced at it in mild annoyance. Wondering if it was a telemarketer, he briefly toyed with the impish idea of answering and putting the caller on an indefinite hold.

Reluctantly he picked up the phone on its third ring.

"Hey Jeff, this is Marty," said the hearty voice on the phone. "Remember me? We had a long conversation at the bar after your keynote speech at that BPM conference."

Jeff's face lit up in pleasure. "Ah yes," he replied. "You were the guy who kept trying to cadge free advice! I enjoyed our discussion! You kept asking all the really tough questions. How you been?"

"Surviving, thanks. I really appreciated getting that opportunity to pick your brains. My boss heard the buzz about process management and he is curious about it. I would like to tap into you for some more advice. Professionally this time, of course."

"Gladly. Just let me know when."

---

[21] This is Jeffrey Sterllings' catchy way of referring to pi calculus (late '80s) and Petri nets (1962), two theories that led to the development of process management methodologies and tools.

"Excellent. I'll set something up for two weeks from now, if that's okay with you."

"I have a scheduled lull coming up around that time, so that works perfectly."

"In the meantime, I'm hoping you could do me a favor."

"Shoot."

"It's like this. The son of a close friend of mine is in an MBA program at the University."

"No crime in that. It will keep him off the streets."

"That's what his father figured. Anyway, they hold a quarterly colloquium where they invite prominent academicians, writers, CXOs, and such like, to come talk to the MBA students."

"Those can be fun events, as long as the speaker is not a boring slide reader."

"I am glad you think so, because this is where you come in."

"I can sense you are setting me up for something. Spit it out!"

"You'll make a sharp detective! Well, their upcoming speaker cancelled at the last minute, claiming he was busy helping authorities on compliance issues."

"Not going to jail, is he?"

"I hope not. Anyway, as you can imagine, this leaves the MBA colloquium organizers in a bind. My friend asked me if I knew anyone who might be able to step in, and I immediately thought of you."

"Why not you?"

"Oh, I think you'd be a more entertaining figure than me."

"Flattery will get me every time. But I am not going to wear a clown outfit. I have to draw the line somewhere."

"If you could just juggle all the current acronyms, that would meet their needs. They are dying to know what the latest technology and management alphabet soup means. If you are agreeable, I'll give the organizer—James St. Royal is his name—your phone number. They are planning an interesting format for the colloquium that should be right up your alley."

"Sounds intriguing! I love talking to MBA students. I especially love talking. As it so happens, I'm taking a break from consulting to work on my book, so I'll be able to help out. I'll wait to hear from James to go over the details. Name the place and the time of the colloquium so I can mark it on my calendar."

Marty told him.

* * *

An interesting medley of aromas jostled for space with the waves of excitement in the packed room. Three matronly tables, set to one side, played host to the several students milling around them. Jeff saw students bending forward, sniffing appreciatively, and peering at small placards. Amused, he marched over to the tables. On each table sat sleek, steaming bowls of soup, serenely perched on tripods, their nether regions gently warmed by small spirit lamps.

The room was packed with about forty students from the regular MBA and the executive MBA programs. A few doctoral students from the Business School and Computer Science also showed up, curious about new corporate fads in IT and management. They wanted to figure out the research angles in any emerging trends.

The meeting room was located in the admissions building. For one week every semester it was packed with harried students going through the exciting ritual of admissions and selection of courses. Guidance counselors, exuding an air of *in loco parentis*, offered advice and soothed the nervous students. At other times, the hall was used for the meetings of the various clubs.

"Hi!" said a voice at Jeff's shoulder.

Jeff turned around. A young man, looking well-scrubbed and studious in his round glasses, stood smiling at him. In contrast to many of the other students circulating about, he had taken some care with his appearance: clean-shaven, slick hair groomed and brushed back, a dark-green collared t-shirt, navy-blue sports blazer with gold cuffs, dark slacks, and Gucci loafers.

The young man shot his cuffs, thrust out a hand, and said, "Hi, you must be Dr. Sterllings. I'm James St. Royal. I'm the chairman of the MBA Colloquium. Or should I have said, 'chairperson,' though that's so politically pretentious, no?"

Jeff waved modestly. "Good to meet you, James. Please call me Jeff."

James looked scandalized. "Oh no, that will not do. We must use your title. All our professors insist on it." He dug a sharp conspiratorial elbow into Jeff's side, and continued in a stage whisper, "Your title will impress the daylights out of these students. It will also keep the poor hungry doctors at bay—that's what we call these Ph.D. students, *PhD*, 'poor hungry doctors,' get it? Heh, heh! Would you believe that a few of our profs showed up? There, look at that guy in the blazer. He's a professor of marketing. That oriental lady over there is an assistant professor of computer science. Do you see that distinguished-looking gentleman in a taupe jacket by the window? He is a professor of DIS/MIS.[22] That gentleman with the goatee is an associate professor from Engineering, though why he turned up I can't imagine. Must be the soup. We formed this Colloquium recently. We meet quarterly, three times a year. Another incongruity, don't you think? A great way for all of us to get together and yak. We're looking for a fantabulous name for our club..."

Jeff lifted a hand to gently stem the flow. "How about *The Loquacious Colloquium*?" he suggested.

"Perfecto! We'll use it. I hereby claim copyright. We will get started on our soup soiree in five minutes. The colloquium members were really eager to know all about the latest ABC's from the real world. I'm glad you provided me a list of acronyms last week when we spoke. See the placard in front of each tureen? That's the description of the soup. There is an acronym on the reverse side. That's one of your acronyms that we'd like you to shed some light on. Alphabet soup, get it? Heh heh!"

James buzzed off to poke and prod at the other students, and to generally liven up things. Jeff wandered over to the soup tables to

---

[22] DIS: Decision & Information Science; MIS: Management Information Science

inspect the samples. The aromas from the soups proved to be a powerful distraction. Within a few minutes, he heard the delicate tinkle of a metal fork against a glass. He looked up and saw a frail student trying to call the meeting to order. He wasn't having much success.

James St. Royal materialized beside the ineffectual student. He clambered up onto a chair and bellowed, "Yo! Pipe down! We need to get cracking. We don't want the soups to evaporate."

Within seconds the student body composed themselves into a semblance of order. Their faces took on a half-amused, expectant look.

"I'll be brief," promised James, warming up to his introduction. The student body groaned. The student body had prior experience with his brief introductions. Undaunted, James plunged ahead.

"Glad you could all join us today. We have here a special guest who will enlighten us about the latest technologies, theories, and whatnot. He comes from a curious background of academics and industry experience..."

James spent the next ten minutes detailing Jeff's career and accomplishments, his introduction unnecessarily lengthened by his opinionated sidebars into technology and management. He lasted a good ten minutes.

"...and now, please join me in welcoming Dr. Jeffrey Sterllings."

Relieved by the termination of James' monologue, the students clapped enthusiastically. Jeff, poised and confident, took a step forward, creating the effect of moving onto center stage. He began easily in a conversational tone that carried far into the hall.

"Thanks for that wonderful introduction, James. I didn't know I had such a varied career! I'm not sure how much I can tell you about the latest technologies, but I'll definitely have opinions about the whatnots."

Appreciative laughter flowed out from the audience.

"I invite you to engage in a dialog with me. I don't believe in monotonic lectures," continued Jeff. This was both a subtle but good-natured dig at James and, with his use of the word 'monotonic,' an inside joke for the mathematically trained students.[23] "During the evening, please feel free to ask me about anything that weighs on your mind. Technology and management-wise, I mean. Ignore politics, wars, and the latest Harry Potter movie."

James St. Royal took over to give instructions for the soiree. "This is an organized soup tasting event," he said, beaming at them and rubbing his hands. "We are going to visit each soup in order. We have a few helpers who will be filling up small plastic bowls with soup and passing them around. The student who prepared the soup will read out the placard that describes the soup. You will then taste the soup. This is not like wine tasting, so don't spit out the soup! When you are done, discard the used plastic bowls and spoons. Then, Dr. Sterllings will decode the acronym that is on the back of that soup's placard and unlock its secrets for us. While that's going on, our helpers will be busy filling up fresh little bowls with the next soup."

The first attraction was a sautéed onion and aubergine soup. A pretty redhead stood in front of the tureen and introduced the soup to the audience.

"Hi, I'm Cynthia. This is a delicate soup that traditionally pcasants enjoyed on Sundays for their dinner. It gave them a break from the heavy soups that they consumed on their workdays. The secret to giving this soup an exotic flavor is in the process of sautéeing the onions and eggplant. The eggplant is then pureed, but not the onions."

A delicious interlude of soup-slurping followed.

Jeff stepped forward and took up the placard. He read out the acronym on the back. "SOA."

A student standing a few feet away on Jeff's left spoke up. "That was my request. I am an MBA student, and I don't think I'll ever write a line of code. I'm curious about all this hoopla over SOA."

---

[23] Students of any discipline that contains advanced mathematics like to talk about a special class of mathematical functions called monotonic functions, which may, on occasion, get monotonous.

"SOA is a good place to start, because that's one of the main villains of the piece in this new technology drama. A lot of the excitement revolves around that. Sometime later I'll introduce the second culprit, called BPM, that is causing some angst and skepticism among executives–at least to those who are reading the signs.

"SOA stands for Service-Oriented Architecture. First of all, let me tell you what it is *not*. The word *service* has nothing to do with customer service. It has even less to do with IT providing services to its internal customers, such as email, web site, network, chat, and iPods. Sad, but there it is. SOA is not a software application. It is not a software package. You can't buy it at your friendly neighborhood computer store. You can't even order it online. Well then, what exactly is it?"

Jeff stood casually and spoke easily. He held each student's eyes briefly before moving on. He took care to engage the people towards the back of the room.

"This may seem like a lot of hot air to you, but SOA is really a philosophy of building applications. The secret ingredient in SOA is the word *service*. It is this underlying method of designing software that gives systems architecture a special, sophisticated flavor. SOA is also a set of tools and technologies that make that philosophy practical. How many of you have any kind of engineering background?"

A few hands went up.

"Excellent. You folks will get this right away, but almost everyone here has seen what the engineers call a *parts explosion* diagram."

There were nods from most of the students.

"A parts explosion diagram takes what may be a compact black box device, and spreads it out in 3D space, with dotted lines to show how the parts connect to each other. It exposes the contents of the black box while preserving its structure. The only time you really get to see this is in an engineering course. Appliance manuals generally have such pictures. When you folks go home, pull out the owner's manual for any of your appliances."

"Especially you men," said a co-ed, looking around impishly.

Gentle laughter floated around the room.

"Now, think about doing a parts explosion on an IT application," proceeded Jeff. "Inside the application, what passes for parts are modules, functions, components, and so on."

"Objects, classes, databases, and things like that?" asked a student from the MIS department.

"Yes, that is correct. Now, in a typical IT shop, you could perform a parts explosion on each of their applications. Almost immediately you'll see something interesting. Can anyone guess what it is?"

A few brave students ventured.

"It's all completely messy?"

"The components are not well-defined?"

"We will find our missing socks?"

"Not quite. Especially not the missing socks, unfortunately! What I think you'll find is that many of the parts are duplicated. Several functions that are almost similar in their functionality are replicated in each computer application. Here is the first principle of SOA: remove common functionality and create a standalone service out of it. Every application that needs that service will call on it to ask for that functionality."

"Isn't that the same as object technology?"

"It is similar, but not quite. I'm simplifying this somewhat, but in object technology you have to follow a certain style of writing code, a style that rigidly binds objects together. The objects themselves could be copied and reused by each programmer. It is not as if one object performed one service. Instead, you might end up with a lot of little clones of one object. In SOA, you don't have to adhere to a coding methodology, with one minor exception. You could write your services in non-object code. What you end up with is the equivalent of one object providing one service. Strictly speaking, your clients shouldn't care how you implement your services, only that you fulfill your published contract."[24]

"You mentioned an exception."

"The exception is that your service should be available to the world at large. That means your clients should have a way to invoke your service. You could insist that your clients speak your language to request service, or you could use a commonly-accepted language and protocol of communication."

"So, it won't work if we all live in a tower of Babel?"

"True. But James is signaling us to move on to the next soup."

A heavy-set, dark-haired young man with a buzz cut stood nervously in front of the next tureen. He cleared his throat and began shyly.

"Er...cooking isn't really my thing. I was tempted to heat up a can of soup, but I guess that would be cheating! So I asked my mom to give me a recipe. She handed me a traditional Italian recipe for minestrone soup, which calls for the addition of smoked sausages and spareribs towards the end. The soup is then simmered for an additional half-hour. Hope you all like it!"

There were admiring grunts and nods as they all tasted the result of the young man's adventurous foray into the kitchen. This time, Jeff drew "EAI" from the back of the placard.

"At the previous tasting, we stopped to discuss the chaos of the tower of Babel. This soup is a great introduction to the next topic. It appears that to make a really good minestrone, the right vegetables in the right proportions must be used. Only then do they all play nicely with each other and contribute to making a tasty delight. It other words, they must be well-integrated. That is the big challenge of Enterprise Application Integration. EAI is concerned with the issue of many applications talking to each other and getting along with each other. Much like the United Nations, the EAI solutions supply translators and brokers to help widely divergent technologies talk to each other. What has changed in the last few years is the widespread acceptance of the hypertext transfer

---

[24] This is the general idea behind component technologies such as COM+ and web services.

protocol, more familiarly known as 'http,' as the preferred method of communicating over the Internet."

"Web services, here we come!" said a lanky student overdressed in a warm jacket.

Jeff laughed and pointed at him. "I swear he's not my plant feeding me segues!" he said. "You are absolutely correct! All the traditional rivals and vendors have no problem accepting two critical technologies of the Internet era: http, and XML. Hence this sudden dawning of a glorious age where applications can talk to each other with this common medium and common language."

"I think I understand this http thing," said an MBA student. "We see it all the time when we browse. What is this XML though?"

"That's a new acronym," observed James St. Royal. "Why don't we wait until we come across its companion soup?"

They moved on and gave a tall brunette their attention.

"Hi everybody," she said, smiling at them engagingly. "This is my grandmother's favorite recipe. She used to whip up this soup on those special occasions when we kids visited her during the summer vacation. The recipe is an ancient one, handed down to us from generations. It is an extra-rich mushroom and leek soup. The extra-richness comes from the rich clam broth that forms the base for this soup."

After tasting it, everyone agreed that the soup recipe should be preserved for many more generations.

James St. Royal read out the acronym chosen to accompany this soup. "What a coincidence!" he exclaimed ingenuously. "The topic of this soup is *XML!*"

"Almost too good a coincidence," observed Jeff, shaking his head with mock suspicion. "XML stands for eXtensible Markup Language. Ignore for a minute what *extensible* means. For you computer science and Ph.D. types, it just means you can construct your own ontologies."

"Dr. Sterllings," interrupted a student. "You used a sixty-four thousand dollar word, *ontology*. What the heck is it?"

"You'll regret asking," said another student standing next to him, shaking his head at his friend.

"I'll explain, but remember, you asked for it," said Jeff, rubbing his hands with glee. "An ontology is an explicit specification of a conceptualization.[25] It comes from two Greek words meaning the 'study of *ontos*, or *being*,' and forms a branch of metaphysics, which is itself a branch of philosophy; in that context, it is a study of *being* qua *being*. However, in computer science and knowledge theory, it stands for a language, or a specification, that describes the entities of the knowledge domain, their attributes, and their structural relationship to each other."

"I'm sorry I asked," said the student dolefully. "I'll stick with the word *ontology*."

"You have my sympathy," said Jeff, reaching out and patting the young man on the shoulder. "What is particularly titillating is that ontology is supposed to clarify the semantics of the domain with which it deals, but the word itself is pretty ambiguous. But let's come back to XML. The critical concept of XML is that it is a way to *markup* your documents with semantics. For example, you could take the text of a soup recipe, and put in tags that say, 'Here be the ingredients, here lieth the cooking procedure," and so on. Using the XML tags as landmarks, a computer program can parse the text to find out where the ingredients and the cooking procedures are. Without such markup, a text document is just so much unintelligible garbage as far as a computer is concerned."

"I don't get that," protested a student. "A text document is not just a meaningless jumble. It has structure and meaning."

"Yes, but only to humans. When you read any document, you mentally assign semantic tags to portions of the document. For example, in an email, you will be able to point out to me where the body begins and ends, and how it can be distinguished from the salutation, despite that fact that a letter does not come with semantic tags. But for a computer, no such general knowledge exists."

"Isn't that the goal of Artificial Intelligence?"

---

[25] www.wikipeida.org

"Absolutely. Unfortunately, that is a very difficult problem to solve. It is much simpler to just tag all documents with semantic clues and let the computer use them to parse the documents."

"Fascinating as all this is, what's it in aid of?" another student wanted to know.

"I'm glad you dragged me back to practicalities! XML allows computers to structure messages that go between them. Using the semantic tags, computers would know how to parse a message. When a web service, which is just a sophisticated computer program, receives a message, it says to itself, 'Oh, here is a request for me to prepare an invoice and send it back; here is the customer number that I have to use to pull the correct data.' Besides knowing the semantic tags, two computer programs don't have to agree about any other formatting, such as using fixed-format files and so on. These semantic tags are what make all documents extra rich in meaning."

"So, what you are saying is that both http and XML contributed to the current explosion in SOA."

"Correct. Remember the first principle of SOA? It was: *create a standalone service[26] out of common functionality.* XML helps implement the second principle of SOA: *use a standard and ubiquitous communication protocol.* It also helps to have high bandwidth available for doing the communicating.[27] More and more people are switching to broadband, so bandwidth is becoming less of an issue now. Most importantly, network bandwidth inside the corporate firewall is not really a bottleneck anymore for most applications."

"But what if I don't want my services available to everybody on the Internet?" asked an executive MBA student. He was an IT manager for a retail chain.

---

[26] These standalone services may be implemented as web services. However, the idea of SOA precedes web services.

[27] XML happens to be a verbose language, and is not the only communication protocol. Performance issues may prevent its usage in situations where large amounts of data need to be transferred between computers, most often between companies.

"There is no requirement that web services be exposed to the outside world. In fact, most services will be made available only inside the corporate firewall. That's perfectly acceptable. However, within your company, you'd still use http on the intranet."[28]

"Are there more principles of SOA?" asked James St. Royal, the Colloquium Coordinator.

"Yes, but I'll share with all of you just one more for now. It is this: even if you have no reuse, it pays to create services for well-defined pieces of functionality."

There were puzzled frowns from the computer science students. One of them objected. "Isn't reuse the true reason for SOA?"

"Yes and no. Reuse is enabled by SOA. But what if you have absolutely no services worthy of reuse. Would you still use SOA? I contend that you should. The reason is that (a) it is difficult to predict in advance when a piece of functionality will see reuse, and (b) cleanly separating functional modules into services makes your testing more manageable."

"What is the net-net of SOA?" asked an executive MBA student. She was the CFO of a pharmaceutical company.

"There are several benefits. Firstly, less code. The amount of reduction depends, of course, on the current state of IT applications in a company. Secondly, faster development, since programmers would reuse some of the pre-existing services. Thirdly, quicker changes. There is a mystical name for this benefit. It's called *agility*. For IT applications, agility means the ability to make very quick changes to applications. If your application is nothing more than a set of distinct services threaded together, you could quickly spot the one service whose behavior needs to change, and you could change it pretty quickly. Fourthly and finally, testing happens to be a major contributor to cost in application development. SOA minimizes testing significantly, especially when

---

[28] An intranet is that portion of a company's computer network that is internal to that company and can only be accessed privately by its employees through a login id and password; in contrast, an extranet is accessible by the company's suppliers, vendors, partners, etc.

you have to change only one small part of the application."

"I think I understand why there is so much excitement about SOA," said the CFO. "Are these principles of SOA well-established?"

"It depends on which methodologist you talk to. Personally, I get the impression that most people who talk about SOA, even those who write computer programs using it, do not realize it is more of a philosophy and a specification than just a bunch of IT tools. But at a high-level, I think this is a pretty significant shift in how applications are built. Some of you will be writing code, while others will be managing technology. For the benefit of both groups, I will leave this subject with one thought: if you work in an internal IT department, don't write code as if you were going to put it in a shrink wrap package and park it on a shelf in a computer store. Your code does not need to be self-contained with its own database, its own reports, its own forms, and such like. Learn to mix and match. Steal and reuse from other internal applications. On the flip side, create your own services in a way that allows your colleagues to reuse them. A critical challenge, of course, is that the available services must be published and accessible through a directory. That is a specialized subject in itself. There, we should now move on to the next topic."

Key Points

- SOA is a philosophy of building software applications by creating small, well-defined programs that follow certain standards to communicate with one another.
- The widespread use of http and XML facilitates SOA; the decreasing cost and increasing speed of networks also helps.
- XML adds meaning to documents and messages.
- Reuse is a powerful incentive for SOA, but even in the absence of reuse, SOA facilitates software quality assurance, testing, maintenance, and enhancement.

3 Enter Stage Right, BPM

James St. Royal shepherded everyone towards the next table. A tall, lanky student, dressed in a professional chef's uniform, stood stiffly in front of the next tureen of soup.

"Hi! I'm François. I want to introduce you to a variation of the mulligatawny soup," said the graduate student, who was majoring in hotel management. "This soup has a history that is very interesting. It originated in India, and is loosely translated as 'pepper-water.' The British adapted it by adding meat to it. The one you will taste now is a variation called blended potato and mulligatawny soup."

The audience tasted the soup and expressed delight that the pepper-water had been thankfully tamed by *l'Anglais*. François, the budding chef, read out the acronym chosen to partner with his soup: 'Bé-Pé-Em,' he called out, his French accent introducing an air of continental sophistication.

"Ah! BPM, the next villain of the piece!" said Jeff. "It stands for *Business Process Management*. But that's like labeling Einstein a physicist. While the concept itself is simple, there are as many angles and perspectives to it as a mangy dog has fleas."

One man standing in the middle of the group waved at Jeff. "I'm a professor in the business school. Would you consider Business Process Management to be a reincarnation of Business Process Reengineering? Are we going to see massive layoffs again?"

"The way people are employed and utilized is outside the scope of BPM. However, there is no dearth of excuses for layoffs. If it is not BPM, it will be SOA, SOX, SARS, Innovation, Agility, Global Competition, Local Competition, and so on. If nothing else, Global Warming will become a convenient scapegoat."

"I thought the message in some of your articles was that BPM helps in smoothing out the hiring curves."

"I'm flattered someone is reading my articles. I give out that message when I'm in one of my more evangelistic moods, when I tend to be overly optimistic about human nature. At these times, I claim that BPM will do away with layoffs because it allows companies to manage recruitment more smoothly. It will do away with the rapid spikes and dips in employment. However, that is a very idealized scenario, and assumes that the culture of process management has permeated the DNA of a company, and that it is coupled with the effective use of technology."

At this point, Jeff led a brief excursion into the reengineering movement started by Hammer and Champy.[29] Animated dialog sparked the air. The audience explored the impact of reengineering, its successes, and its failures. Jeff related a personal story.

"I once led a process reengineering effort more than a decade ago for a telecom company down south," he said. "The company wanted to consolidate all of their billing processes. It was a clean-up project to prepare them for the anticipated Telecommunications Act that would promote open competition between local and long-distance providers. Besides, utilities would be able to get into the telco markets as well. Suddenly, it promised to become a free-for-all. My story is not about the process methodology or the technology we used. It is about the human dimension. The subject matter experts on the team were very perceptive about the meaning of reengineering. They demonstrated true professionalism on the project, but one engineer clearly told me, 'I know I am reengineering myself out of a job. Guess what? After work hours, I'm reengineering my resume.' Until he made that comment, I was a naïve technologist and process methodologist."

"No wonder you emphasize the cultural aspects of BPM so much," said another professor.

"Yes. That incident really opened my eyes to the organizational impact of any new technology or methodology. After I think I have a handle on whatever new thing comes along, I make it a point to ask myself, *How will this affect the people? How will their behavior change? How will the behavior of their manager and their HR department change? How will incentives be aligned with the new processes? What will the employees*

---

[29] *Reengineering the Corporation: A Manifesto for Business Revolution*, Michael Hammer and James Champy

do on a daily, tactical basis? How will the planning and budgeting processes change? Specifically, BPM forces collaboration and communication across former boundaries. SOA's success depends on how well we plan for reuse and on how well we design systems that transcend functional boundaries. It may seem ironic that new ideas such as BPM and SOA, while solving one set of problems, bring to the surface a host of others. However, I consider these new problems to be of a higher-order, or of a more enlightened kind. In any case, I can assure you that the insights offered by this line of questioning can be illuminating."

James St. Royal asked, "Dr. Sterllings, you mentioned BPM has many angles. Could you please elaborate?"

"Definitely. The first and the most necessary aspect of BPM is the process modeling. Without process modeling, nothing will get off the ground."

"What additional value-add can BPM provide to process modeling compared to existing tools like Visio?" challenged one professor of marketing. "Visio is pretty widely available and well-known. That is an unbeatable advantage."

"That's like saying cigarettes are widely available and everyone knows how to smoke, so they have an advantage. Having an advantage is not the same thing as being the right advantage. Indiscriminate use of Visio has hampered productivity. It has created too many process silos. It has proliferated flexibility to the detriment of standardization. Remember, Visio is in fact an excellent tool for drawing out a great variety of maps and models, but it was not exactly designed with process *management* in mind."

"Of course, Microsoft may come up with a BPM-compatible Visio version," observed a professor of computer science.

"True. BPM, on the other hand, promotes standardization. The notation used by BPM is called BPMN, or *Business Process Modeling Notation*. It eliminates the headache of having too many process mapping symbols to choose from."

"BPMN has a very limited set of symbols, though. Isn't that a problem?" asked a computer science graduate student.

"Yes, the symbols are limited, but that's actually a good thing.

I've been process mapping for two decades now. I have not yet had the need for anything beyond the handful of symbols that are defined in BPMN. Now, that covers process modeling. Next in the sequence is process analysis. Here, there are two types of analyses: one is based on statistics, and the other is non-statistical in nature."

"By statistical analysis you mean Six Sigma?"

"Affirmative. However, Six Sigma is more than a set of statistical techniques. It includes numerous tools that are used to manage change in organization. The non-statistical techniques include LEAN and process maturity metrics. None of these analytical techniques are exclusionary; there is no need to choose one and exclude the other. A fluid mix of analytical models can be employed. This is an interesting, but vast, subject in its own right, so we should move on to untangling some of the other acronyms."

"Are we still on the subject of BPM, Dr. Sterllings, or are we moving onto pure technology?" asked a young woman standing right in front of Jeff. She had pulled out a small notepad from her jacket, and was consulting it.

Jeff glanced at her notebook. "Looks like you have a list of acronyms that you want me to cover, right? Okay, let me know if, by the end of our discussion, I do not cover anything on your list."

James St. Royal assumed control.

"The next table has all bisque soups. These are thick soups with pureed seafood. Some of the braver students, under the guidance of François, created their own recipes to loosely match some of the acronyms we'd like Dr. Sterllings to cover. We had to name them inventively in Franglais, a mixture of French and English, so please be indulgent!"

Jeff chimed in with his own interpretation of the forthcoming delights. "Soups are nutritious because they contain many vitamins, among other nutrients. One of the more complex vitamins are the B-vitamins, also called the B-complex. BPM has its own equivalent of B-acronyms. I suspect we are about to discover some of them."

Their first stop was a bisque de roasted eel.

Jeff turned towards the audience. "BRE stands for *Business Rules Engine*, an application that allows you to specify business rules in a way that can be linked to real data within your other applications and that can be executed."

"Are these the same as inference-based rule engines?" asked a computer science student.

"Yes, though each implementation may have its own flavor of expression and execution. For example, the engine may parse rules expressed as "if-then-else" statements, or read antecedent-consequent expressions. Execution may follow either a forward-chaining or a backward-chaining strategy. Similar to a BRE, there is also a BPE, but am I running ahead of the soups?" asked Jeff, raising an eyebrow towards the next soup stop.

Predictably, the next soup turned out to be bisque pea with egg-drop.

"As I was about to say," continued Jeff, after they had spent a few happy minutes tasting it, "BPE, or *Business Process Engine*, executes the processes themselves, much as the BRE interprets business rules."

"The BPE sounds like a computer operating system," commented a doctoral student from computer engineering.

"That is correct. I want to clarify one term that we keep bandying about with no clear definition. I refer to the word 'process.' We have quite a few computer science students here who are used to thinking of 'process' as an element of an operating system. In computer science, a process is an instance of a running program. The operating system manages all these processes and the inter-process communications. This meaning of the term 'process' is very different from that used in BPM, where it refers to the representation of a business process. This representation is a static picture of how the business operates. A Business Process Engine converts this process—a static picture of a business process—into a computer program, and executes it as a dynamic process that is under the management control of the engine. The BPE itself is a computer application that runs as a process under the management of the computer's operating system. Is all this complicated enough for you?"

The audience chuckled at Jeff's dexterity in navigating through the maze of process semantics.

The next presenter was an assistant professor of computer science that Jeff had seen earlier.

"The soup I prepared is also a bisque, with asparagus and mussel," she said. "Since I am from Hong Kong, I garnished it lightly with spices sautéed in sesame oil. I hope you all like it."

Her willing guinea pigs agreed that this was one soup they had never tasted before.

"Anyone guess what the next topic on our list would be?" asked Jeff.

The co-ed in the front with the list helped him out. "I guess it would be BAM."

"Good guess," verified Jeff, looking at the back of the plaque. "BAM is pretty explosive! It stands for Business Activity Monitoring. It is George Orwell's 1984. It is the big brother breathing down the neck of each business process. It is the cop lying in wait for speeding motorists. Technically, it is an application that keeps watch over business processes that are running under a BPE."

"What exactly is the BAM application watching? I thought the BPE manages the processes."

"The BPE manages processes by firing off code that implements process steps, manages data flow between steps, invokes adapters to third-party applications, and invokes a BRE to implement decision paths and also to execute decision steps within process steps. Finally, it handles the start, the stop, and the exceptions. The BAM engine, on the other hand, checks for control points or key performance indicators that have been defined as part of the process mapping exercise. When these control conditions are met, the specified triggers are fired off. Notifications may be sent out, colors may turn red on digital dashboards, or other applications may be invoked."

"So everything has to be specified up front?" an MBA student minoring in finance wanted to know.

"Not everything. A good BAM engine monitors the flow of business transactions throughout the process and provides any number of metrics, such as throughput, cycle time, average, variance, and so on. The control points that I talked about are those that are of special interest or specific to a business process."

"I am not sure I see the connection between creating a business process and its execution," said an MBA student. "How does that transformation happen?"

"Shall we wait for the right soup to come along and help us digest that difficult topic?" asked Jeff.

That was the cue for the group to move on to the next item on the buffet. James' helpers moved efficiently, getting the soups ladled out for all before the completion of the previous tasting.

François came to the fore again. "This one is a complicated soup, so I made it myself. I had to do it twice, because the first time it did not turn out correct." He waved towards a bubbling tureen with a flourish. "Messieurs et mesdames, voila! Bisque Potage Mushroom Neapolitaine!"

Everyone looked suitably impressed. The flavors were complex and clearly justified a four-word title for this soup.

Jeff picked up the baton after a five-minute Neapolitan interlude. "Here is an excellent way to understand the connection between creating a business process and executing it. State of the art BPM tools will provide you the BPMN modeling toolset to help you create a standards-based process model. BPMN stands for *Business Process Modeling Notation*. The BPM platform may also contain simulation tools that will allow you to analyze the performance of processes. The platform may also capture various kinds of information about your processes; some may even allow you to hyperlink web pages, documents, and so on. All of this is an excellent value in itself. Some BPM packages then take you to the next level. They translate your pictorial model that you described using BPMN, into a computer-friendly specification called BPEL, which stands for *Business Process Execution Language*. Think of BPEL as the partial code of your business process. BPEL is in fact written in XML."

"Extensible Markup Language," James St. Royal reminded them helpfully. "I am certain that our next soup was designed to help you explain BPEL."

"Bisque pepper lobster," announced an executive MBA student. "Light on the pepper of course. The eel and the eggplant were already taken, so I had to make pepper contribute two letters to this acronym, Dr. Sterllings. I think you were going to enlighten us about BPEL."

"Thank you. As you may know by now, an XML document is simply a text file, not a formatted one like an MS Word document. BPEL, as I mentioned before, is an XML document. You could read it, but a complex BPEL document wouldn't make much sense to you, as it is chock-full of technical tags such as link-types and port-types. Besides, it's more verbose than a professor of elocution."

Jeff paused, wondering if he had offended anyone. He was reassured to see that even the faculty had joined in the laughter.

"Where does this BPEL document go? What's the next step?" asked another student.

"The BPEL document is a computer-friendly specification of the business process. Our good friend, the BPE, or Business Process Engine, understands BPEL. Various tools can be used by developers to fill in the gaps. For example, a process step may call for a certain type of processing. That processing capability may lie within an existing application, like an inventory management application. The programmers would know how to take the XML specification and write code to connect to that application, usually using adapters."

"But what if that functionality does not reside in any of the existing applications."

"In that case, the programmers would write custom code to supply that functionality. Ideally, they'd write it as a web service. Remember our other friend, the SOA? After writing the web service, they would hook it up to the rest of the BPEL. The BPE takes in all this information and executes it."

"Looks like many things have to come together to make all this work," observed James St. Royal. "I mean, there are so many opportunities to get things wrong."

"Not necessarily. The risks are minimized by making sure that the tools and technologies at every step are based on some standards, such as BPMN or BPEL. However, in one sense you are correct. Not all vendors implement standards in exactly the same way, just as no two orchestras play the same symphony in exactly the same way. Vendors interpret standards differently. Sometimes this is deliberate, because they want to differentiate themselves. At other times, it is unintentional because the standards are specified in a general way to allow for flexibility and future development."

"Then there are custom enhancements to standards," offered a professor of computer science.

"That complicates the picture. There is no true competitive advantage to just implementing a standard. So, vendors tack on additional features, much as two performances of a particular concerto may have different cadenzas. Also, the standards themselves are evolving. In practice, care must be exercised if you are going to mix and match technologies. This piece of practical wisdom holds true in general, not just for BPM."

"Is there any easy way out from this, apart from just ignoring BPM entirely? In my entire professional life, I've never seen a solution to this problem." The speaker was a veteran computer science professor.

"Well, companies shouldn't really ignore BPM. It behooves management and technology professionals to keep an eye out for new ideas. While not all of them pan out, the risk of missing something truly useful is high if you don't keep up. Some vendors realized that the risks of matching and mixing provided them a good opportunity for creating and offering a consolidated suite of these various BPM-related modules. This gave birth to BPMS, the *Business Process Management System*." Jeff paused, and turned towards James St. Royal. "Does that merit another soup?"

"Unfortunately, Dr. Sterllings, we are out of soups! BPEL was the last one we ate," replied James from the other end of the room.

"That's probably as well," said one computer science professor. "I couldn't have eaten anymore."

The co-ed with the little notepad asked, "Dr. Sterllings, would this BPMS be a convenient packaging of all the modules? Would each module follow the same standard or the particular interpretation of the standard, all having access to the same custom extension, and so on."

"That is the theory. But, TANSTAAFL![30] What you gain in convenience you lose through vendor lock-in and dependence."

James St. Royal, who had made been hovering around the edges, now briskly strode up to stand beside Jeff.

"This has been very interesting and informative. I know you are all burning with questions. Unfortunately this hall is reserved for the remainder of the evening for the meeting of the local history chapter. I have been asked to announce that they'll be discussing the influence of the Borgias on the Renaissance, just in case anyone here is interested. Anyway, we'll have to vacate the premises now. The Colloquium will host a happy hour at Bertie's Bar. So, if you have any questions and wish to discuss more, please swing by to Bertie's in fifteen minutes. Would you like to make a closing remark, Dr. Sterllings?"

"Indeed I would. There are many domains that touch BPM that we did not cover today. Knowledge management is one of the most important issues in the corporate world. Document management is another, which is surprising considering how we are always about to go paperless. Compliance is an extremely critical issue today. You've been reading the news and browsing the Internet, so I won't belabor this point. BPM is not a replacement for these specific systems. However, it can significantly help by tying knowledge, documents, and compliance control points to business processes. As you can see, process management is a field that touches many aspects of corporate life. I want to leave a couple of takeaways for you—put them in a doggie bag if you will.

"One, process management is not a new fad: it is the result of serious work by academics and thought leaders for over three

---

[30] There Ain't No Such Thing As A Free Lunch. The acronym, now used as a word, was introduced and popularized by the famous science-fiction writer, Robert Heinlein, in his book, *The Moon is a Harsh Mistress*.

decades. Two, process management is by no means mature: it is subject to rapid evolution, intense research, and redefinition of terminology. There is considerable posturing, differentiating, and consolidation of vendor offerings. Three, even though we covered many technical topics, process management is not primarily a technology issue: it is essentially an issue of management and organizational culture, with significant ramifications for implementation within IT; be aware of this as you continue your exploration of BPM. Four, process management is itself a process, recursively speaking: buying and implementing a BPM system is not the complete solution.

"Thanks for having me on your menu tonight. I'm always energized when I talk at academic campuses. If I left out any of the B-acronyms, please catch me at Bertie's Bar. Just don't order any Borgia soups!"

Key Points

- BPM is not the same as business process re-engineering or a new way to downsize corporations.
- Because BPM provides better visibility on how people support processes, it helps in hiring, on-boarding, training, right-sizing, and retaining employees.
- BPM impacts the organizational processes and corporate culture including strategic planning, budgeting, tracking business measures, and tactical behavioral changes.
- The first and most necessary aspect of BPM is process modeling and analysis; Business Process Modeling Notation is a process documentation standard.
- Six Sigma provides tools for statistical analysis of processes; BPM enables sophisticated non-statistical analysis of processes.
- Business rules can be better managed and implemented by Business Rule Engines.
- Business Process Engine automates business processes; Business Process Execution Language is a standard for documenting the executable model of a process.
- Business Activity Monitoring deals with keeping an eye on processes as they execute, alerting or notifying someone when exceptions or errors occur.
- XML is a popular standard that forms the basis for BPMN, BPEL, and other process-related specifications.
- BPM facilitates the solution of many of the important corporate problems, such as knowledge management, document management, compliance, and controllership.

4 Will BPM Deep Six Six Sigma?

It was one p.m. on an early winter afternoon. There were a few joggers huffing and puffing along the pathways in the park, while many more were taking what was called, in a more leisurely era, a 'constitutional.' Jeffrey Sterllings pulled out his pipe and set it beside him on the park bench. Reaching into his coat pocket, he extracted a pouch of Prince Phillips pipe tobacco. He set this beside his pipe. This was followed by a long slim case of pipe filters. Finally, he looked around vaguely, patted himself all over, located his matchbox and extricated it from an inner pocket.

There was a crunch of footsteps. He looked up and saw a chunky man in his mid-forties trudging towards him. Jeffrey waved at him in recognition. The man responded with a hearty, "Hi!"

Jeff stood up, and they shook hands.

"Good to see you again," said the newcomer. "How have you been keeping?"

"Very enthused, Marty, very enthused. Lots of neat things happening. How's life treating you?"

Marty Montrose gave a grunt of dissatisfaction. "Fine, I suppose, all things considered. Thanks for helping my friend's son, James St. Royal, with his MBA Colloquium."

"My pleasure. How is work? When we spoke on the phone, you gave me the impression that you had problems."

Marty snorted. "Who doesn't? You solve one and then you got another. Problems are like a bloody hydra."

"Be glad there are problems, Marty. Without them, folks like you and me would be out of jobs."

"There's that, of course," said Marty, chuckling. His mood was lightening rapidly.

Jeff moved his pipe paraphernalia to make room for Marty on the park bench. As Marty settled down at one end, Jeff busied himself with lighting his pipe. Fascinated, Marty watched the three-minute ritual that had all the exotic elegance of a Japanese tea ceremony. Having satisfactorily assembled a fully functional pipe, Jeff struck a match, cupped his hands around the bowl, and lit the tobacco. Small puffs of smoke punctuated the air around his lips in a steady beat, giving the impression of a mini steam engine pulling out of a train station.

Jeff leaned back, a contented smile on his face.

"Now," he said, waving his pipe. "What's bothering you?"

"I know you are a hot shot in Business Process Management. I heard you speak at that BPM conference. How are you on Six Sigma?"

"Not so hot."

"I was afraid of that."

"I am only trained as a Six Sigma black belt."

Marty raised an eyebrow. "Oh, setting a pretty high standard there, aren't you? Anyway, I'm glad you 'fessed up to some knowledge of Six Sigma. I'm a little confused about whether BPM and Six Sigma show up at the same party."

"Believe it or not, I get asked this sometimes. Not only do they show up at the same dance, they also tango together very well."

"I was hoping you'd explain the moves."

"I take it that this is not a purely academic question?"

"No, it's not. My boss asked me to look into this BPM thing. He wants to make sure we really need it. Our Head of PIQ, Process Improvement and Quality, is saying, 'We already have Six Sigma, so why do we need a competing methodology to improve business processes?'"

"That is a very common reaction. I see that all the time."

"Is BPM threatening Six Sigma? Is this becoming a turf issue?"

"As long as there is any misunderstanding about BPM, it will end up becoming a turf issue. BPM does not threaten Six Sigma, anymore than an airplane threatens a car. BPM complements Six Sigma."

"You have to explain that to me," said Marty, grumpily. "When our Head of PIQ made those statements, I had no answer for him. I didn't know which way to look."

"How did you leave it with him then?"

"I said that I completely agreed with him that we do not need a competing methodology. However, I added, I wanted to make sure that we are not missing something. I told him that if I could find enough evidence that BPM offers more than Six Sigma, I was sure he'd be the first to fight for it."

Jeff let out a chuckle. "Good maneuvering there, Marty. You're getting to be a savvy corporate politician."

Marty gave him a wry grin. "My donkey is still on the line, of course. I have to prove that BPM is Six Sigma Plus."

"If you are looking for proof that BPM is a turbo-charged version of Six Sigma, I'm afraid I'll have to disappoint you."

"Oh, I understand," said Marty, hastily. "When I say proof, I don't mean in the mathematical or the legal sense. A fairly decent argument with a few supporting facts should be enough. After all, the Head of PIQ is a reasonable man."

Jeff sighed. "Maybe I should restate what I said. If you are looking for even a shred of argument that BPM is super-Six-Sigma, I can't help you."

Marty's face fell. "Oh! And I thought you were a passionate BPM evangelist."

"I am," said Jeff, taking a pull on his pipe. "Before you jump off your tenth floor office, here comes the cavalry. You are looking for the wrong argument. You are trying to convince yourself and your Head of PIQ that BPM is the slicker version of Six Sigma. In fact, BPM does not even compete with Six Sigma. The two are dimensionally different."

"Though I am partial to the marines, I'll take the cavalry when I can. Enlighten me, O BPM sage!"

"I didn't know they had corporate classes on sarcasm," retorted Jeff, tapping his pipe on the bench. "Very well. How good is your Six Sigma knowledge?"

Marty shuddered. "I was never any good at statistics."

"Seems like a lot of stutterings[31] to you, eh? Statistical analysis is the key underpinning of Six Sigma. To make hard-core statistical

---

[31] Charles Dickens, "Hard Times."

analysis palatable and usable in the corporate world, some of the pioneering companies surrounded it with a framework, a methodology, and a culture. DMAIC[32] and Lean[33] are easier to pronounce and grasp than 'Tests of Hypotheses' and 'ANOVA.'[34] It is easier to certify someone as a black belt than to certify them as a Junior Statistician. Regardless of all the surrounding wrappers, Six Sigma at heart is a statistical discipline. Take away the statistics and what are you left with?"

"A jelly-doughnut with all the jelly sucked out of it?"

"Exactly. Did you have lunch yet?" Jeff lighted his pipe once more and continued. "BPM is radically different. BPM is not only a framework and a methodology, but also a set of tools to manage processes."

"Wait! The same can be said of Six Sigma. So what's different about BPM?"

"The same *cannot* be said of Six Sigma. Six Sigma does not manage processes. It gives you a set of pretty sophisticated tools to analyze them from a statistical aspect."

Marty tucked in one leg on the park bench and turned fully toward Jeff. He was excited. "Hot ziggity! Six Sigma is a subset of BPM!"

"You make it sound rather inferior, like a second class citizen. It's more like an honorary adjunct faculty to the BPM department. BPM gives you one more way of analyzing processes rather than only focusing on statistical analysis."

"Cold ziggity. You lost me on that one."

Jeff marshaled his thoughts, gazing into the distance, the intensity of his eyes flickering behind the wisps of smoke.

---

[32] Define, Measure, Analyze, Improve, Control: one of the Six Sigma methodologies.

[33] Also known as *Lean Manufacturing*, it is a philosophy of process improvement that focuses on elimination of waste or wasteful activities. Though Lean originated in the context of manufacturing, it has been extended to cover business processes in general.

[34] Analysis of Variance: a set of statistical tools to compare two or more means (i.e., a type of 'average') by investigating the underlying variance.

"The biggest shortcoming of the Six Sigma framework," he resumed, "is that it does not deal with the information architecture of processes, the different categories of data that can be associated with processes. Hence, it does not have a sophisticated toolkit to document processes in standard forms, or to build process models that are easily translatable into IT implementations."

"It does too! Our PIQ organization uses Visio."

"Congratulations! They are one step ahead of the miserable folk who use PowerPoint to draw their processes. But suppose you asked your PIQ department the following questions: What roles perform the most manual steps throughout the organization? How many handoffs occur in order processing? On average, how many process steps does your CRM solution perform in a given customer service process before handing control of the process over to your back-end ERP[35] system? Hmmm?"

"I asked everyone in my company similar questions. I have an easy answer: nobody knows."

"'Nobody Knows The Trouble I've Seen,'" sang out Jeff in a strong tenor. Marty joined him in solemn baritone. They broke off in laughter when they got to "Hallelujah!"

"Seriously, tell me," said Jeff. "If your PIQ organization recommended *increasing* the number of handoffs to reduce cycle time, would your management buy into it?"

"Most likely, though I'd find it tough to believe they'd recommend that. Let's be fair. My PIQ organization is not incompetent. If anything, they are an excellent group."

"I'm not questioning their competence. I'm only pointing out that their charter is limited in scope, by design and by necessity. Their charter is to seek what mathematicians call local optima. It is well known in the mathematical world that a set of local optima do not necessarily make a global optimum."

---

[35] Enterprise Resource Planning: also referred to as "back-office" systems, ERP usually denotes a very large application package or a very large set of applications that performs many critical functions such as logistics, billing, invoicing, warehousing, accounting, and human resource management.

"I'm supposed to nod intelligently at that statement. After all, I took graduate math. But what in gobbledygook's name are you talking about?"

"Just this: a Six Sigma black belt selects a small, well-scoped process to improve. Within six months (if they are following DMAIC) or within two months (if they are following LEAN), they come up with an improved process. Perhaps they end up reducing defects by one sigma level, which is commendable. Their 'local' process is now optimal, let us say. Does that necessarily make the larger process optimal?"

Marty was thoughtful. "I see what you mean. A few years ago, we optimized one of our originations processes by eliminating what we thought were redundant audit procedures. We later found out that our risk management discipline had slipped. A couple of deals that shouldn't have been approved got funded. We just wrote off a good chunk of money last month on those deals. In a similar vein, we decreased the design cycle time for one of our products, but it adversely affected the service and repair. So, BPM is supposed to prevent this sort of fiasco?"

"Not automatically, no. No more than using Six Sigma will guarantee that you will reduce your defects. Nothing can substitute for human analysis and judgment. BPM provides you the tools and the methodology that could force you to consider the big picture."

"Okay, I'll take that on faith for now. So, in the brave new world of BPM, who would do process improvement?"

"I'll answer that question if you answer mine. Pick any non-trivial business process in your company. Who is that one individual who knows everything about it?"

"I don't think there would be any one person."

"So, the answer to your question about who would do process improvement is: everyone. But you are peeping into chapter two, figuratively speaking. Chapter one is about capturing and documenting the current process. BPM provides you a framework and a set of tools that force the issue of capturing processes in an information-rich way. We can discuss what that really means at a later time. But the point is that no one person or group has all the information about non-trivial business processes. If they do, you are asking for big trouble. BPM tools allow various parties to record their knowledge of the process and thus create one common model of the business process. Different parties can view the aspects of the process model that are relevant to their job."

"You mentioned the figurative chapter two? Are we there yet?"

Jeff looked at his watch. "That's a big topic. But briefly, analysis of processes can occur from the standpoint of classical Six Sigma, such as cycle time, mean, variance, number of defects (or its converse, the yield), and so on. BPM augments that from a different standpoint. It introduces the concept of process maturity metrics. The two types of analyses complement each other and allow for better decision-making. BPM ensures that other people besides those in Six Sigma provide an input into process improvement. And here's the clincher: the effort to do both kinds of analyses is synergistic, not accretive."

"I'll have to look up those words."

"Why don't you do that, hmmm? My pipe's out. That's my signal to head back to work. If there is one takeaway for you from all this conversation, it would be what I modestly call *Sterlling's Theorem on Six Sigma*: 'BPM synergistically complements Six Sigma.' It has a corollary: Six Sigma experts will NOT be out of a job."

"You'll dispense more wisdom the next time we meet, yes?" asked Marty, hopefully. He was busily making notes.

"Definitely. Allow me to give you the distinct pleasure of buying me lunch next week."

"Any particular restaurant?"

"Yes. The kind where they serve food."

Key Points

- Six Sigma is a specialized discipline that provides sophisticated statistical tools to analyze processes.
- Six Sigma does not manage processes, facilitate non-statistical process analysis, or translate process improvement plans into IT models.
- The focus of Six Sigma is to improve processes so that they become locally optimal.
- BPM forces people to consider the non-local consequences of processes.
- BPM allows specification of processes that are easily translatable into IT designs.
- BPM complements and extends Six Sigma in the analysis and improvement of processes; BPM includes non-statistical metrics to analyze, monitor, and manage processes.

5 The Omniscient Process

Jeffrey Sterllings sauntered out of the local bookstore. He paused for a moment, glanced around absent-mindedly, then set off in one direction with a decisive step. It was unusually warm for this time of the year. The air was redolent with a sharp lemony tang, suggestive of freshly scrubbed furniture. Naked beams of stark silvery sunlight wove a warm fabric that shimmered and enveloped, simulating a security blanket. The happy hordes, seduced out onto the streets by the clear skies and luminous light, jostled and bustled about with purpose writ large on their faces. They seemed intent on practicing the hoary dictum, *carpe diem.*

Within a few minutes of brisk walking, Jeff met up with his friend, Marty Montrose, who was waiting for him at a busy intersection, glancing at his watch pointedly.

"Not late, am I?" asked Jeff. "Good," he continued, without waiting for an answer. "Let's find a place to eat. Where are you taking me?" he asked, rubbing his hands with suppressed glee.

"I rather fancy Italian," said Marty, mildly put out for not getting an apology from Jeff for being tardy.

"Excellent choice," replied Jeff. He steered Marty gently but firmly towards a restaurant that was currently the rage. It was part of a Japanese restaurant chain called MICO. Each restaurant was cunningly placed either right across from a TGIF or in close vicinity to it. For people in the know, MICO was a reverse-acronym that stood for 'Oh Crap! It's Monday.'

Marty groaned. He knew he would be all thumbs with his chopsticks. "Found something interesting at the bookstore?" he asked indiscreetly.

Jeff pulled a book out from its paper cover with the air of a kid showing off a brand new toy. It was titled, 'Learn Hiragana.'

"What is that? Animal, vegetable, or mineral?" asked Marty.

"Sorry, none of the above. It is one of the scripts of the Japanese language."

"I'd never have guessed. There's more than one script?"

"There are three. Hiragana is the 'traditional' Japanese script. The Chinese kanji, the ideograms, are also adopted by the Japanese. Finally, they use Katakana to write words of foreign origin."

"Whatever for?" asked Marty, totally mystified.

"If you tell me, we'll both know."

Marty looked like he had blundered into the twilight zone. "You mean to tell me you bought a book on one of the Japanese scripts without knowing why?"

"Oh, I thought you asked me why the Japanese have three scripts. That, I don't know. I do know why I bought the book. Because I want to teach myself Japanese. Let's just say it is a hobby of mine."

"Er...that's very commendable. Now, about the BPM issue we talked about..."

"What's interesting," continued Jeff relentlessly, as they got seated, "is the amount of information the Japanese have to learn in order to communicate in writing. In English we make do with 26 letters of the alphabet. The Japanese have to contend with two sets of 56 letters each, one for Hiragana and one for Katakana. Technically speaking, Hiragana and Katakana are not alphabet sets. Rather, they are syllabaries. To make life complicated, they also use Chinese ideograms, called 'Kanji.' So, in addition to Hiragana and Katakana, schoolchildren are expected to master about 1200 Kanji characters by their senior year."

"Makes you wonder why our kids, with only English to grapple with, can't get their spellings right."

They dug into their soba noodles. Jeff wielded his chopsticks expertly with all the finesse of a gentleman samurai. Marty's bowl ate more than Marty did.

"English is linguistically efficient," said Jeff, clicking his chopsticks together in emphasis, "while languages like Japanese and Chinese are semantically richer. The challenge is to strike the right balance. This is critically important in a BPM platform, since the information stored in an information-rich process has multiple uses and many audiences."

"You are now on the subject of information architecture in

BPM, I take it?" asked Marty, vainly chasing his noodles around in the bowl; he was reminded of the time when he tried to catch fish in a garden pond with his bare hands.

"Quite. See how dexterously I weaved it into the conversation?"

"You were definitely more deft with your argument than I am with my noodles."

"Use a fork, for heaven's sake. That reminds me," said Jeff, waggling his fingers at a passing waitress. "Saké! Arigato!"

"So, tell me more about this information architecture," Marty suggested, wiping his chin.

"You told me on the phone that your Head of PIQ complained that a process methodology forces users to capture way too much information."

"True. He did not see the point of gathering all that data. He said they'd never use it all. All he cared about was mean, variance, and cycle time."

"The PIQ folks—we should call them the PIQers—may not use all that information, but other business users would. Your IT professionals would use quite a lot of it. Think about it! Every time you start a new project, what is the first thing you do?"

"Conduct user interviews and define requirements?"

"No."

"Get funding for the project?"

"No."

"Get sponsorship?"

"No."

"I give up."

"Assess where you stand. Determine what your current process looks like. Figure out what your applications do. Without all that, you have no idea how to estimate the size of the problem. You can't estimate the cost in order to make a funding request. You can't ask for sponsorship if you can't explain credibly what you have and what you don't have in terms of functionality."

"Yes, of course. It was so obvious I missed it."

"What kinds of information do you think you would need to make a fairly decent assessment?"

A soft sibilant sine wave acoustically announced to the world at large that Marty was sipping his soup.

"The actual process itself, of course," he ventured, "and the nature of the transactions that flow through it. In fact, we frequently get into arguments about data fields and their meaning. So, metadata would be very useful. Information about how each process step changes a transaction, or how it might change the data fields, or how it might compute, transform, or derive other data. That kind of information would be invaluable."

"How about roles? The *who does what?*" prodded Jeff.

"That as well."

"How about locations? The *who does what where?*"

"Ditto."

"How about which line of business or P&L is impacted? Which functional organization has ownership for a task?"

"Likewise," said Marty, signaling for the check.

"Now, what if, at the start of a new project, you had all this information available to you?"

"It would be terrific. We would know exactly where we stood. We wouldn't yet know what needs to be done, but the pieces of knowledge about roles, locations, transactions, data fields, etc. are pretty useful."

"If you had implemented BPM a year ago, and followed the methodology with good discipline, that is exactly what you'd have at your disposal now."

"But gathering all this information takes a lot of time! We can't execute our projects on schedule as it is!"

"That's because, during your requirements-gathering phase, you are spending a lot of time on what I call 'discovery of current state.' You just can't avoid going after this information. You either do it when the right audience is available, captive, and reasonably energized at the start of your project, or you are forced to do it later when everyone is tired of the sight of you. At the start of your project, your subject matter experts, your PIQ experts, and your IT analysts are all gathered in one large room. The CIO and business sponsors have just left the room after cutting the ribbon and having kicked-off the proceedings. They expect that the worker bees will roll up their sleeves and sweat out the nitty-gritty. Why not document the project's business process in all its glory and semantic richness once and for all, and be done with it? Hmmm?"

"Your 'pay me now or pay me later' argument is persuasive."

"It's reality," said Jeff, pounding the table and making the dishes jump. "You can't shortchange reality with impunity. TANSTAAFL, as Robert Heinlen put it."

"Tan what? Robert who?"

"TANSTAAFL stands for 'There Ain't No Such Thing As A Free Lunch.' This principle, while universally recognized, was immortalized by this acronym by the late science fiction writer, Robert Heinlein."

"I thought we IT guys only recognized TLAs."

"Speak for yourself. I am not just an IT guy. Anyway, TANSTAAFL is a concatenation of three three-letter acronyms. That symmetry, the devious numerological pattern, should tickle you."

"I am ecstatic. Where is that waiter with the check?" asked Marty, irritably. They had been waiting several minutes to pay their bill.

Marty turned his attention back to information architecture. He scratched his chin thoughtfully with his useless chopsticks. "Most of the time we can't even find the process maps we built last year. It's a crying shame, because a bunch of really talented people spent oodles of time analyzing and documenting them."

"Most likely they used PowerPoint or Visio to draw their processes, printed them, and filed them away somewhere. This is exactly the kind of waste and inefficiency that a good BPM platform will help you avoid. Actually, there's even more information we can collect and assign to processes. This information will be useful for extended analysis throughout the lifetime of the business process.

"You also get one unexpected benefit which, now that I mentioned it to you, will not be unexpected anymore: all the information you thus collect will smoothly transition into the future-state map, or what is called the "to-be" process map. This could be used to build your training material. You could publish your process map and associated documentation, allowing your users to view the new process, the business rules that are to be employed to execute the process steps, the various roles performing them, the identification of risk and control points, and so on. But that is a deep topic that we can explore later."

"I see the light now. It is important to collect as much relevant information as possible about a process when it is fresh in peoples' minds."

Jeff had no intention of letting Marty have the last word. He stood up and stepped onto his chair. People at the neighboring tables gawked. Marty's eyes widened.

Jeff said, "If there is one take away from this conversation, it is my formal expression of TANSTAAFL. I humbly call it, Sterllings' Law of the Conservation of the Cost of Information: *The cost of collecting and documenting information is constant in any given context, but the consequences of not collecting it multiply the longer it is delayed.* It has a corollary: *Make your process documentation as information-rich as you can as early as you can, and you shall be freed from an impoverished analysis.*"

"What are you doing?" asked Marty nervously, for Jeff had remained standing on his chair, perfectly composed, while he delivered his sermon to a restaurant that became increasingly quiet. Everyone stared at Jeff and made hushed comments to each other. A nervous snigger broke out at a distant table, and was quickly stifled. The harried head honcho came hurrying by, accompanied by an entourage of waiters, ushers, and chefs.

"Anything the matter, sir?" he asked Jeff.

"Not at all. We'd just like the check, please," said Jeff suavely.

They were out of the restaurant in record time.

"Thanks for a lovely lunch, Marty. Good choice of restaurant."

"You're welcome," said Marty, drily. "By the way, what would you have done if your tactic of standing on the chair hadn't worked?"

"I'd have escalated."

"Meaning?"

"I'd have stood on the table."

Key Points

- Information architecture refers to a comprehensive way to capture different categories of data that are associated with processes, such as cycle time, variance, business rules, data flows, process metrics, throughput, people, roles, etc.
- Discovering the current state of processes and systems is a time-intensive activity; lack of knowledge management makes the discovery phase very inefficient.
- BPM has the tools that document, categorize, analyze, and maintain knowledge about processes and systems.

6 A Process on the Freudian Couch

Once upon a time there was a process called Underwriting Audit. He was a sad process, because all his so-called friends nicknamed him 'Undie.' That was not the worst of it, though. He got a reputation for being a mean, ornery process who found fault with everyone. They even made up a little ditty about him, singing at him as he passed by in a huff:

> *The process called Undie*
> *Is as messed up as Ted Bundy.*
> *He hacks and he sacks,*
> *Calls the rest of us lax,*
> *And is more of a pain than Mrs. Grundy.*

He did have a few supporters–'friends' would be a bit of a stretch–who knew that he kept the rest of the processes in line. His supporters, mostly senior managers, called him 'Rite,' because they said he knew right from wrong.

No, he was not wholly sad because of the silly nickname or the ridiculous limerick. He was depressed because he was all confused inside his head. He had no sense of identity, no clear understanding of who he was or what his role in life was. He was frequently asked all kinds of questions by senior managers, but he had no ready answers. The junior employees asked him why he did what he did, or why he behaved in a certain way, and he had no clue. He usually retorted, "That's policy! That's how I have to do my job. It's nothing personal, see?"

But they didn't see, of course. They wanted logical explanations–as if logic mattered in business! He wanted to have friends, to build some meaningful relationships, but he found that impossible. Other processes were unapproachable. He seemed to be an island unto himself. He suspected that the other processes were also islands, and he wished he could somehow help them. But corporate policy dictated that he constantly criticize them, hover over them, waiting for them to make a mistake and slip up.

No sir, he was not a happy process at all. He couldn't go on like this. Why, just the other day, while waiting for the train at the subway, he caught himself wondering how it would feel to throw himself onto the tracks in front of an oncoming locomotive.

He knew the time had come to go and consult a shrink. A hollow laugh of bitter irony escaped his lips. He, the product of a LEAN workout, was going to the shrink!

***

Dr. Jeffrey Sterllings leaned back in his chair, his fingers forming a steeple in front of his nose, a slight frown furrowed on his smooth forehead, as he looked at his patient over the top of his glasses. He was a tall man in his mid-forties, with a good head of unkempt hair. His face was all angles. His corporate clients sent him their confused and muddled-up processes. He helped these unfortunate processes get untangled, simplifying their lives enormously, improving their relationships with other processes, and helping them lead long, productive, and happy lives.

Mr. Audit lay on the couch on his back, one hand thrown across his eyes, sobbing softly. He held soggy tissues in the other hand, and dabbed his eyes ineffectually from time to time.

"Mr. Audit," said Dr. Sterllings, softly, "would you like to tell me how you are feeling?"

"I feel like terminating!" sobbed poor Mr. Audit. "You don't know the pressure! The nature of my job makes me unpopular. They all hate me. But if it were not for me, their undisciplined behavior could cause our company enormous losses. Why don't they understand that?"

"What makes you think they don't understand the importance of what you do?"

"For starters, they call me names," said Mr. Audit. He shared with Dr. Sterllings the nickname they had given him, and with burning cheeks recited the disgraceful ditty.

"It gets especially terrible at fiscal close!" he continued, keening dismally. "Everyone, including the senior management who normally support me, wants to shove me aside. They don't let me do my job. They say I hold up the transactions when, in reality, they are the ones making all the mistakes."

"I think I can help you resolve these issues. Let's start with a psychological test, okay? I'm going to show you some pictures. You tell me what you see in them, all right?"

Dr. Sterllings pulled out a plaque. A Rorschach ink-blot was pasted on it. Subjects were supposed to name the object or objects that the ink-blot evoked in their minds.

"Come, wipe your eyes! Tell me what you see here, Mr. Audit," said Dr. Sterllings, gently.

Mr. Audit squinted at the plaque.

"That looks like an ink blot," he ventured tentatively.

Dr. Sterllings' jaw tightened. This was going to be difficult.

"Yes," he said, managing a gentle tone. "I know that. What does it remind you of? What everyday object comes to your mind when you look at it?"

"Decision boxes," said Mr. Audit, this time more confidently.

Aha! thought Dr. Sterllings, *now we are getting somewhere.*

"How about this one?" he asked, producing another ink-blot.

"Branchings."

"This one?"

"Multiple paths."

"Now we'll go on to a different exercise. I'll mention a word. Say the first word that comes to your mind when you hear it. Don't think about it. Let's start. Okay?"

"Crazy."

"No, no," said Dr. Sterllings. "I did not start yet. *Now* we start. Rectangle."

"Failure," said Mr. Audit promptly.

"Path."

"Split."

Dr. Sterllings scratched his chin. "Start," he barked.

"Stop."

"Begin."

"End."

"Diamond."

"Problem."

Dr. Sterllings was silent for a few moments. He was mulling over Mr. Audit's responses.

"I see," he began, having formulated his diagnosis.

"Darkness," cried out Mr. Audit.

"No, no," said Dr. Sterllings, more sharply than he intended. "We are done with the word association exercise. I can now tell you what your problem is. I see that you suffer from a narcissistic, neurotic, manic-depressive self-absorption, leading to diadikasiophobic multiple-schizophrenia."

"Huh?" Mr. Audit was pleasantly surprised. This sounded very important and impressive. And all this time he thought he had been suffering from a run-of-the-mill depression.

"Let me put it more simply. You suffer from overly complex, self-referential, multiple, bi-directional graphs leading to frequent and abnormal terminations."

"Huh?" Mr. Audit was doubly impressed. Even the explanation of the diagnosis sounded suitably intimidating.

"Let me put it even more simply," said Dr. Sterllings. "Too much thinkum makes you crackum."

"Oh! What's the cure-um?"

Dr. Sterllings wiped his febrile brow.

"Let's analyze this first before opening the medicine cabinet."

He led Mr. Audit away from the couch and seated him informally in the corner sofa. He poured them both cups of steaming coffee.

"Now, do you know how many steps there are in what you do?"

"Let's see," said Mr. Audit, holding up the fingers of one hand. He began counting, and promptly ran out of fingers. "Of course," he said, reflectively, "I have a few subprocesses. Three? No, I think five. But the fourth one is not really my subprocess. It is a D&B check." He was referring to the Dun & Bradstreet company information service. "Maybe it really *is* my subprocess. So perhaps I really do have five subprocesses. No, wait, what about the 'verify pricing' subprocess? That would be the sixth, though I think the 'verify pricing' subprocess is actually a child process of the 'verify economics' subprocess. Do you really want me to count *all* the process steps that I have? Do you want me to include the process steps in all my subprocesses, and *their* subprocesses?"

"Do you think that would be helpful?" asked Dr. Sterllings. "Do you think if you had an inventory of your process steps you would start getting a handle on who you are?"

"Yes, I think so. Unfortunately, I don't really know all the steps I perform. I don't even know with certainty who my children are, not to speak of who *their* children are. I am really confused," said Mr. Audit, unhappily.

"I think we should take that as an action item for your therapy. I know it will be difficult, but trust me, you'll feel a whole lot better when you know."

"But how can I take an inventory of all my processes?" asked Mr. Audit, desperately. "I tried that last year when I felt really blue. I documented as many steps as I could discover. I used several A4 size papers and taped them all up on a wall to figure out how my process flows looked."

"So where is that map now? Why aren't you referring to it whenever you feel confused and depressed?"

"Oh, it got unwieldy. I got my process steps changed so often that I couldn't keep up with the changes anymore, so I gave up."

"Did you find out that someone else influenced your children to change their behavior without your knowledge?"

"How did you guess?"

Dr. Sterllings sighed. "I've seen too many cases like yours. I know all the problem spots."

"So how do we fix that, doc?"

"I'll give you a prescription at the end of our session. Now, let's continue our investigation. Do you know how many decision points you have?"

Mr. Audit closed his eyes and tried to count. His face contorted furiously as he tried to keep pace with the branches and loops that ran through his head like a clutch of hyperactive snakes. After five minutes of making horrible grimaces and twisting himself into shapes that dedicated yogis would have found challenging, he gave up on his mental–and physical–gymnastics.

Changing strategy, he spent another five minutes scribbling furiously on a number of pages, drawing complicated diagrams full of branches and probabilities. He gave that up as well when he found he had about a dozen messy pages strewn about, with no hope of assembling them into any semblance of order. He sat there, amid the chaos of rumpled papers, a dazed and distant look on his face.

"Well? Did you figure out how many decision points you have?" asked Dr. Sterllings, gently.

"Eh?" said Mr. Audit, slowing pulling himself together. "Not really," he declared, sniffling sadly.

"Don't worry, we know how to fix it. But before we apply the poultice, do you really believe deep down that a knowledge of your decision points will make you a happier person?"

"I think it would help, but I have a feeling I should know a lot more than that. Is it really possible to get to know all my decision points and the resulting branches?"

"Absolutely! It takes the right medicine and the right discipline. You also need patience. But it can be done. But before I prescribe the medicine, I need to know more about how self-aware you are. Do you know how many end-to-end paths are possible within your entire process?"

Mr. Audit closed his eyes, and started tracing in the air with his hands. After a couple of minutes, Dr. Sterllings interrupted him.

"Would it be safe to say," he asked, "that you really have no clue?"

Mr. Audit looked deflated. "Yes," he admitted. "You would be quite safe in saying that."

"Just as I thought. How's your knowledge of all the roles employed in all the tasks that you do?"

"Again, I know a few, but I can't give you a definitive answer."

"Just as I suspected. Do you know how many process steps on average any of your roles perform?"

"I don't even know what you are talking about."

"Just as I surmised. Do you know how many IT systems and applications you use to perform your job?"

"If you tell me we'll both know."

"Just as I hypothesized. If I asked you how many steps each of your applications perform on average, what would you say?"

"I would request that you please speak English."

"Just as I conjectured. Then I won't pose that question to you. How's your governance?"

"He's doing fine. He recently got re-elected."

"Not your governor, your *governance*. If any of your children misbehave, do you know about it? What do you do about it?"

"I wouldn't be able to recognize some of my children if I passed them on the street. I don't even know how many I have at any given moment. How can I know what they are doing? My risk-exposure subprocess—assuming she is my child—could be doing a strip-tease for all I know."

"Just as I assumed. You lack the capability to do a simple, single dimensional analysis of the contents of your consciousness."

"That bad, eh, doc? How long have I got?"

"I don't think you are a terminal case. You could survive for years without a total breakdown."

"That's supposed to console me? I think that's a worse fate. I'd rather end it all now."

"Take heart! I have successfully helped many processes like you. I am very confident I have a cure for you. My formula will improve your mind, smoothen your relationships with the other processes, and make you the envy of all processkind."

"Okay, doc. Where's the magic elixir?"

"The most important ingredient of the ambrosia is your ambition to improve yourself. Are you truly motivated to uncomplicate your life? Are you serious about finding lasting happiness? Do you really want to slim down and be able to turn on a dime? Think before you answer, because the cure will not be easy. It will require vision, commitment, and patience. The problems are deep-rooted, so the cure is by necessity also deep. It *can* be done, but you *must* truly want it."

"Yes, yes, and a thousand times, yes! Let's do it doc!"

"Excellent! That's the spirit! I've mapped out a regimen for you. Let's meet regularly every week and review our progress."

Dr. Sterllings wrote on his prescription pad, tore out the sheet, and gave it to Mr. Audit with a flourish.

Mr. Underwriting Audit looked at the paper with burning curiosity. Dr. Sterllings had scrawled on it, in his inimitable sprawling hand, the following prescription:

Bepium, qty365, tid.
Unlimited refills

Key Points

- BPM offers the tools that allow processes to be self-descriptive.
- Using a BPM platform it is easy to build dashboards that monitor the health of processes, and to supply tools that allow analysts to query processes about their behavior.
- BPM allows analysts to understand the relationships between processes, thereby determining how process changes propagate throughout the company.
- A good BPM platform helps in the governance and controllership of processes.

7 Equanimity with Equations

Jeffrey Sterllings looked at his old mentor fondly. Professor Feinstein had aged quite a bit since the last time they met. The shock of thick white hair seemed more unruly than ever. The face was pinched and wrinkled. But the professor still had the same impish smile, the same twinkle in his eye, and the same sharp brain that nourished his catholic interests.

"It's good of you to spare me the time, Professor."

"Alfred to you, my boy, Alfred. It's good of you to come and visit an old man."

"Thank you, Alfred. I would have come sooner, but it seemed profane to bother you with trivial issues when you are toying with monumental theories."

"Toying? Struggling is more like it."

"I can't believe you'd struggle with anything. What are you working on these days?"

The professor lit an odious cigar.

"I'm working on the most elusive social theory of all: a unified theory of social interactions. We know how to characterize political interactions; we know how to model individual rational behavior; we also know what makes a group of people in a bar behave the way they do. Some of these interactions are weak social forces, and some are strong social forces, but we scientists are having a tough time coming up with one single model that'll explain it all."

With characteristic humility, the Professor did not mention his own singular contribution to social science: the Theory of Social Relativity, which stated in rigorous mathematical formalism that the farther one's relatives lived, the greater the total satisfaction of all parties.

Jeff said, "Sounds very challenging. I'm confident you'll crack it, Alfred."

"I certainly hope to do so before I maximize the satisfaction of my relatives by moving off into the infinite Void. Now, tell me what you are working on. You sounded very excited on the phone."

Jeff couldn't stand the professor's cigar any longer. He decided to fight back with his pipe. He eschewed his usual leisurely routine and lit it with undignified haste.

"For a number of years, as you know from our intermittent conversations," he began, after taking a deeply satisfying pull on his pipe, "I've been working in the field of Business Process Management and Service-Oriented Architecture. Similar to the problem you are facing in unifying the various forces of social interaction, I'm faced with the challenge of coming up with one single model that explains the interaction between BPM and SOA."

"I know you always talk about those subjects when you call me, but my mind keeps wandering off into tension calculus[36] that I employ to model my theories. So you'll have to recap for me what the issue is."

"Gladly. Service-Oriented Architecture is a philosophy of writing software and building systems in such a way that the completed system is a loosely-coupled conglomeration of well-behaved, well-specified, and well-understood blocks."

"Lego blocks."

"Exactly. The analogy with Lego breaks down after that in two ways. Firstly, unlike in a Lego model, one can easily replace components if and when better ones come along, without unduly disturbing or rebuilding the model. Secondly, the same component can be simultaneously reused by a number of applications."

"Sounds wonderful. What's the problem?" asked the professor, waggling his white, bushy eyebrows and tapping his cigar, like an ancient Groucho Marx.

"It turns out that we don't necessarily know what the right modules are, or how they correspond to business processes."

"You mean, your model may not have a one-to-one correspondence with reality."

---

[36] The reader may be excused for thinking this is a typo for 'tensor calculus,' a mathematical technique that was instrumental in the development of Einstein's Theory of Relativity.

"Precisely. So, some of the leading practitioners like myself are realizing that one can't start building services willy-nilly. We have to go back to get a deeper understanding of reality. In our case, the reality happens to be the business process."

"Sounds like the right approach. So, what's the problem?" The professor sent an odious plume of cigar smoke in Jeff's direction.

Jeff countered with a puff from his pipe.

"It seems that on one hand we have a bunch of process designers who know how to model processes very well, and on the other hand we have a gang of coffee-quaffing coders with twitching fingers just itching to write Java, C#, and C++."

"So why don't you just pair up a process designer with a coder. They'll work in tandem. Problem solved. Now, get out and let me get back to deeper problems."

"Not so fast. It so happens that process designers and coders are not always spatially or temporally co-located."

Prof. Alfred Feinstein sighed in exasperation. "Why is it that everyone feels compelled to talk to me in highbrow language? Just the other day, the cashier at our University cafeteria said to me, 'Hello Professor! Change is everywhere. It is driven by entropy, which is time's arrow. Here's your change: 67 cents, a prime number for a prime professor.' Turned out that she was a physics major, working part-time in the cafeteria. She wanted to impress me so I'd get her a regular assistantship. I wonder what ghastly experiments she is conducting at the cafeteria with anchovy and ice-cream. Heaven forbid, she may even get Schrödinger's cat to taste her creations!"

"Sorry, Alfred. I merely meant that process designers and developers do not always work in the same location, because many companies distribute their teams across the globe."

"And that blather about 'temporal co-location?' What's that?"

"Ah, yes. Process designers model processes long before application developers get to them. Even if I can put them in the same cube, one of them would be very busy while the other one would get bone idle at any point in time."

"Seems to me you need a good communication model."

"Absolutely correct."

"Good. Go get a communication mechanism. Problem solved. Now, vamoose and let me flex my neurons on tension calculus."

"In a minute. The issue is that process designers are great communicators. Sometimes you can't get them to shut up. However, developers…that's another story. Let's just say they're 'linguistically challenged.' Most times you can't get them to open up."

"I see you are determined to make this challenging for me. We scientists faced this problem and solved it centuries ago. We decided to use an unambiguous vehicle for communication. We call it 'mathematics.' I hope this doesn't come as a surprise to you, but we scientists are all over the map when it comes to our communication ability. Take me, for instance. I get lingual diarrhea on just about any topic. Now my colleague down the hall won't utter a syllable unless you stand on your head outside her office for a whole year. But if I shoot across a mathematical proposition to her, she'll send me back a counter-example, which amounts to a rejection, pretty quickly. Leastways, it's mostly rejections I get nowadays, and not many acceptances."

"You know I couldn't possibly use mathematics to document business requirements."

"Maybe not, but the more rigorously you document all the information about the process in as standard a format as you can, the better will the communication be."

"We have just such a framework," said Jeff, triumphantly. "It's called XML, a content markup language that, like your mathematics, is universally accepted and understood, by both carbon-based life forms and silicon-based life forms."

"You couldn't just say, 'people and computers,' could you? I wish you'd leave the fancy language to us professors."

"Sorry, close proximity to a professor rubs off on me. Anyway, we let process designers merrily model away using graphical tools. Then, our tool platform converts those models into XML representations. The developer's tool platform also talks XML. So it can import an XML model and convert that to code fragments. The developer merely steps in and tweaks the code if necessary. I am simplifying the picture somewhat, but those are the essential steps."

Prof. Feinstein scratched his chin thoughtfully. "I understand you are keeping the technology part simple for my sake. But, without knowing the details, I'd guess your challenge will be to use a consistent model or formulation. Let me give you a simple analogy. Mathematicians can describe geometric models using either the Cartesian or the polar coordinate system. Depending on the problem or based on personal choice, results in one system can be transformed to the other. This is well-known to mathematicians and does not cause them any grief. I'm assuming that, not having the same maturity and precision as mathematics, information technology would benefit from a standard way to model the architecture of the system."

"Your intuition is remarkable. Technologists realize that we need a way to specify the model of the system in a technology-neutral way. To put it another way, we shouldn't have to use the language of any particular implementation technology.[37] Hence, a method of describing architecture, called Model-Driven Architecture, is gaining ground. It offers an abstraction layer between the specification of requirements of the system and its implementation architecture. As such, MDA is the lingua-franca of systems architecture."

"Okay, so we scientists use math, you use XML and MDA. Each to his own poison. So, what's the problem?"

"The problem is that we don't have a feedback loop. When conditions change, applications detect it first, since all transactions flow through applications in real-time. But they need to translate the changes back to the business processes so that the process owners and management folks can be alerted."

The professor chewed on his cheroot thoughtfully.

"What you need is some form of XML inverse. Or maybe an SOA inverse. You remember your inverse functions, don't you?"

"Absolutely. Our SOA happens to have an inverse of sorts. It's

---

[37] Examples of implementation technologies include .NET and J2EE.

called BAM, which stands for Business Activity Monitoring. It's like a control feedback loop. Engineers use it all the time to maintain environmental homeostasis."

"Remember the space program?" reminisced Professor Feinstein. "It was before your time, of course. Control theory, or cybernetics as it was known then, wasn't yet well established. Deterministic Newtonian mechanics ruled the day. Some scientists even said that going to the moon would be impossible, because the set of mathematical equations that modeled space flight were intractable. They didn't realize control theory would come to the rescue."

"BAM is like that control theory. A dashboard of control metrics would record variations in transaction flows. Since the control points were defined in the original process model, the deviations from the norm could be traced to specific business processes."

"And how is corrective action taken?"

"Well, in one of two ways. The immediate reaction would be to employ a tactical solution. For example, when a company gets an unusual number of deals to finance, the control metric that tracks customer-established turnaround time would begin to get out of whack. The operations manager could then redeploy the operations staff to handle the increased flow until things returned to normal.

"The strategic approach comes in when the abnormal starts to become the normal. Then, the process needs to be re-engineered. Or more people may be hired. In any case, a new process gives rise to new models, and possibly changes to the systems themselves. This brings the systems back in line to reflect the new process."

"It sounds like a neat little ecosystem. Now, you came in here complaining about problems. Every time we try to pin it down, you also seem to have a solution. Interesting as all this is, why are you bothering me with this?"

"It wasn't my intention to ask you to help me create a solution from scratch for all of these issues. What I wanted was validation from you about the interaction between BPM, SOA, and BAM—a validation of the meta-model, if you will."

"Well, so far, it sounds like the whole thing hangs together pretty well. Your only challenge is to make sure the tools that you use along the way know how to talk to each other. The people in this ecosystem must know what their role is, and how they should behave. They should all be trained in this new methodology. For example, they should learn to think in terms of control points when they are designing their processes."

"True. There is one last thing I'd like to get your feedback on."

"I'm afraid to ask, but what is that?"

"I came up with an equation to describe this ecosystem. I framed it in terms of moving from a current state to a future state."

"Okay, sounds intriguing. Shoot."

Jeff walked over to the professor's whiteboard and absentmindedly erased all the intricate formulae on it.

"That's right," called out Professor Feinstein. "Go ahead and erase the only written copy of a highly promising theorem in my unified theory of social interactions."

Jeff whirled around, aghast.

"Just kidding," said Alfred, convulsing in laughter. "You don't think I'd let a precious theorem sit on the whiteboard without a backup, would you?"

"You got me there! Don't do that again. Next time, go ahead and joke about my house being on fire. That, I can take. I wouldn't survive the loss of a theorem."

Alfred continued to splutter in merriment. Jeff, ignoring him, scribbled out his monumental discovery. When he was done, he turned around and showed off his formula proudly:

Let 'F' stand for Future_State,
let 'C' stand for Current_State,
then,
$$F = C * (SOA^{BPM} + BAM * BPM)$$

There was an abrupt silence as Professor Alfred Feinstein switched off his laughter.

"Well, what do you think, Alfred?" asked Jeff, eager as a schoolboy showing off his exemplary report card to a stern parent.

Prof. Feinstein slowly struggled to his feet, stretched out a hand, and walked over to the whiteboard. The two men shook hands warmly for several moments. The professor's eyes were misty.

"So you did learn something after all, my boy! I'm proud of you!"

* * *

"This is too deep for me. What on earth does it mean anyway?" asked Marty. They were sitting outside at a sidewalk bistro, cradling hot cups of coffee in their hands. A piece of notepaper containing Jeff's proud equation rested between them. A porcelain sugar bowl served as a paperweight, while occasional whiffs of breeze teased the corners of the paper.

"Come now, this is no more complicated than middle-school algebra. Tell me what happens if we have no BPM."

"Well, if there is no BPM, we could put zero in its place."

"Good. What will that do to each of the terms in the equation?"

"Let's see, the term 'BAM multiplied by BPM' becomes zero, because any number multiplied by zero equals zero."

"Excellent! Continue."

"Alright. Now on to the term that has the SOA in it. Anything raised to the power of zero becomes zero."

"Not quite."

"Oh, sorry! Anything raised to the power of zero equals one."

"Not exactly," said Jeff, in his best pedantic tone. "Any nonzero number raised to the power of zero equals one."

"That's what I meant," said Marty, and continued hastily, "so, the term 'SOA raised to the power of BPM' boils down to one."

Jeff winced. "*Boils down* is not exactly a mathematical way of stating a result, but never mind. So you have two operands separated by a '+' operator. What is '1+0'?"

"Surprise me," said Marty, clearly annoyed. "I do have a graduate degree, you know, so let me cut to the chase. The result of all these mathematical gyrations is that, without BPM, the *Future State* equals the *Current State*."

"Marvelous. Regardless of what you do in the SOA space, you can't really change the current state without BPM."

"That's mathematics. But is it reality?"

"The math merely makes a dramatic point. Of course, implementing SOA in a void will have some effect, but maybe not what you'd expect, and most certainly with not as much impact as you'd like. Remember what I said at that conference on process management that you attended? Don't start with SOA. Tackle BPM first."

"I can think of one more argument why we should work on BPM first," said Marty, his eyes fulgent with sudden insight. "Not all projects have a digitization component to them. So, by using the BPM methodology and tools, we provide immediate benefit to the business. Any further benefits that may come as a result of implementation through SOA will be gravy on top."

"Now you are beginning to talk like me."

"Scary thought, that! What did your professor think of all this."

"He told me my time and money were well spent at college. I think he's pleased that my equation is almost as elegant as his own in the theory of social relativity."

"Remind me what that is. This is a gap in my education."

"Marty! What did they teach you in college? Ask for your money back!" said Jeff, simulating a theatrical shock. "Prof. Feinstein discovered that the one social constant in the universe is the dislike of one's mother-in-law. He used 'M' to denote the energy of this dislike. He used the letter 'c' to denote the distance between oneself and one's relatives, and the letter 'E' to denote the energy of satisfaction in a relationship. His monumental discovery was the equation: $E = M c^2$. So, the farther your relatives are from you, the happier you'll be. You'll have the least satisfaction, which is the same as saying you'll be most unhappy, when your mother-in-law is at zero distance away from you, meaning, practically in your face."

Marty shuddered. "I completely agree with that. But you were going to tell me all about feedback loops, control points, business activity monitoring, and how the whole edifice keeps a process from going bananas."

Jeff threw a meaningful look at his pipe.

"I know, I know," interrupted Marty. "Your pipe is out, so our session's up. If you went into psychiatry, I wonder if you'd charge by the pipeful or by the hour. You would probably say, 'Sorry, you're pipe's up. We'll have to continue your therapy at our next session.' Would you accept payment in pipe tobacco?"

"Only if it is the best."

Marty edged out of his seat. "Till next time, then," he said, trying to make a quick getaway, but Jeff gestured imperiously.

"Hold on," he said. "I must give you a takeaway for the road. I offer you the Sterllings' Law of State Transition: *A current state transitions into a future state by the application of SOA to a positive value of BPM.* It has a Corollary: *Send your IT folks on a holiday to Hawaii until you hire process designers.*"

Key Points

- While process management and service-oriented architecture (SOA) are independent domains, they can be combined synergistically to produce tremendous leverage.
- The digitization of processes is one, and only one, aspect of BPM; other key areas are process documentation, analysis, knowledge management, process management, and process monitoring.
- SOA is a philosophy of developing software services in a way that would allow them to be flexibly combined and reused to build various applications.
- BPM provides a mechanism to link the technical services of SOA to business process, thus eliminating the IT-business divide.
- Business activity monitoring (BAM) provides operations managers and senior management the ability to monitor the state of their business in close to real-time.
- When BAM is an integral part of a good BPM platform, managers have the capability to control the flow of business processes, and modify them to deal with rapid changes.

8 The Yellow Brick Road to Innovation

They were all assembled in the large board room on an early, chilly December morning. Outside, tiny swirls of snow pirouetted gracefully, resting for a few moments between every bout of the fickle wind. Inside the conference room, trays of continental breakfast and hot coffee were enticingly spread out.

The door swung open, and a tall figure, swaddled in a great coat and hat, briskly strode in. The man flung open his coat recklessly, exploding a mini-shower of snow around him. People standing nearby hastily covered their coffee cups with their hands. The newcomer tossed his coat neatly onto a coat rack, and in one smooth motion set his hat on a peg. He turned towards the people in the room and introduced himself, "Jeffrey Sterllings."

He unerringly picked out the CEO from among the group, and strode towards him with an outstretched hand. Introductions were quickly performed. Dr. Sterllings, or Jeff as he preferred to be called, helped himself to a cup of coffee while the rest arranged themselves around the table. The steam from his coffee cup swirled in sympathetic resonance with the dance of the snow outside.

A projector whirred into action, throwing out a chiaroscuro of light onto a white screen. Marty Montrose, the VP of Information Technology, operated a laptop with the MS PowerPoint presentation that had been sent to him earlier by Jeff.

Jeff looked at the assembled company and smiled at them blandly. "Are we waiting for anyone, or shall we begin?" he asked.

Marty looked around for confirmatory nods, and said, "I think everyone who needs to be here is here. We can begin."

He cleared his throat and continued, "I'll start us off, since I called this meeting. You all know how we are trying to revitalize our IT department. You were all involved in the discussions we have had on consolidating our systems, reducing costs, speeding up development time, being more responsive to rapidly changing needs of the business, and so on. I've invited Jeff to share his ideas with us on how to achieve all this in the most effective manner. I've known Jeff now for several months. I first met him at a conference in California, where he showed up for his keynote address in beach shorts and t-shirt."

There were gentle chuckles.

"I made up for that sartorial faux-pas by showing up for a beach party in Florida in a full suit," said Jeff.

The gentle chuckles morphed into full-throated laughter. Several people leaned back and sipped their coffee appreciatively.

Marty continued, "Since our first meeting, we have been in contact frequently. I have tapped into Jeff's expertise on a number of subjects. Our foray into Business Intelligence, for example, was due to the influence of Jeff."

"The credit for all the costs of BI goes to Marty, of course," quipped Jeff.

"The reason I've asked him to come today is to hear his views on some of the more sophisticated technologies now making the rounds. These are the bunch of technologies cryptically known as SOA, BPM, BAM, EAI, BRE, and so on. Barry, did you want to add anything, or speak about your expectations for this meeting."

Barry Attwater, the CEO, cleared his throat.

"Thanks, Marty. As you all know, I'm committed to investing in new ideas. For the first few years of our existence as a company, we were in a niche market, where we had no price pressure. Unfortunately, we are now becoming a commodity business. Only two courses of action are open to us now, and they are not mutually exclusive. We have to innovate like crazy to maintain our differentiation, and we have to manage our costs diligently. I have had one conversation on the phone with Jeff last week that Marty arranged. Jeff said a couple of things that really impressed me.

"The first point that we should all take to heart is that managing costs is a mindset. Jeff said, *A good manager does not wake up one day and decide to manage costs. Cost management has to be an ongoing exercise.*"

"I wish I had really said that," interrupted Jeff. "I was repeating Warren Buffett's immortal words."

Jeff was referring to the words of the widely-quoted Sage of

Omaha: "The really good manager does not wake up in the morning and say, 'This is the day I'm going to cut costs,' anymore than he wakes up and decides to practice breathing."[38]

"Those are darn good words, I say!" exclaimed Barry. "I couldn't agree more. The other thing that Jeff said struck a chord in me. Our most important resource is not our financing, our set of products, our patents, our sales strategy, or any of the things we usually talk about. The most important resource is our mind. Jeff, why don't you talk about that? You put it so much better."

"Thanks Barry. I wish I had actually said that one too," said Jeff, sadly. "However, Ayn Rand beat me to it. She was discussing the source of the wealth of nations. She contended that the usual suspects, such as an abundance of natural resources or strong armies, are not the key producers of wealth. In fact, the key resource is the human mind. Fortunately, it is the only inexhaustible resource we have available. I totally agree with that. The only thing I'd add is that the human mind must have the time and freedom to think and pursue innovative ideas. The most important resource is not only the human mind, but more importantly, its faculty of attention."

Jeff walked over to Barry's side, and laid a hand on his shoulder. "Barry, tell me. How much time did you spend launching your company ten years ago?"

"Too much time, I can tell you! But I enjoyed every minute of it. It was the most exciting period of my life!"

"How much time do you now spend in developing your company and going after new ideas?"

"Too little time, sad to say!"

"Exactly! What happened between then and now, Barry? What do you do most of the day?"

"Run the business, of course. Deal with customers. Handle problem employees. Ride herd on my team. Approve expenses. File reports. Talk to analysts. You know, the usual stuff."

"And how much time do you spend on dreaming up new ideas and developing them? Hmmm? How about the rest of you?" asked

---

[38] Warren Buffett, in *Fortune*, April 11, 1988

Jeff, casually sauntering about the room and holding each individual's eyes.

"I'd be lucky if I can spend an hour a month on dreaming up new ideas," said Barry.

"He gets to spend an occasional hour on new ideas because he delegates all the heavy, boring stuff to us," said Mark Andersen, VP of Marketing.

"He manages to delegate tasks to us on a Friday evening, too!" chimed Carl Sanders, the Chief of Operations.

Good-natured laughter ricocheted off the walls.

"Whatever happened to TGIF, eh?" retorted Jeff. "Seriously, what could you do with one additional hour every day? How about one additional day a week? Not to waste it on routine meetings, not to call more customers, not to perform more administrative tasks, not to do any of the things you do everyday, but to just sit back and think?"

"I'd probably catch up on my sleep," said Marty.

"You'd deserve it," said Barry. "I know you guys come in on weekends to launch new applications."

"Does that mean you'll approve my request for a sofa in my office?" asked Marty.

"Never!"

As the general laughter subsided, a somber voice piped up, accompanied by clicking sounds. It was Dan "the Midas" Manning, the CFO, punching keys on his calculator.

"If I assume you are talking about us being more productive so that we can accomplish in seven hours what now takes us eight hours, that'd free up about 260 hours every year. So, for every eight people who are thusly productive, we can eliminate one headcount. Given our current number of employees, we can eliminate 418.333 employees, or actually, 418 employees, because you can't eliminate 0.333 employees, he-he-he! At a fully loaded annual cost of, say $104K per employee, that would save us, let us see…approximately $43,472,000 per annum, every annum. I'm keeping my math simple, of course."

There was a shocked silence around the room.

"I've never known you to keep your math simple, Midas," said Barry shakily, after some time. "Are you sure you didn't add an additional zero somewhere? Or multiply when you should be have added?"

Dan drew himself up. "There's no question of error, unless my HP calculator is faulty," he said stiffly.

"All right, all right! Don't get your coin rolls unwound! We would have to generate a sales revenue of close to half billion to generate that kind of net income. Folks, keep this conversation confined to this room. I have no intention of laying off 418 people, and I don't want our discussion interpreted like that."

Jeff quickly intervened. "Before you go gaga over the numbers," he said, "let me suggest a couple of ways of looking at this situation. Your company is still in a growth mode, though, from what I gather, your growth curve is slowing down from twenty-somethings to the upper teens. Right now, I don't think you are very scalable. A tip-off is that like many companies in your situation, your managers have the mindset that the way to handle growth is to simply hire more employees. I realize that sometimes that is the correct way to handle growth, but I challenge the tendency to assume it automatically. I know from my earlier conversation with Barry that your costs have only lagged your income growth by a few percentage points. I'd hazard a guess and say that you are looking to hire about 400 people next year. Would that be in the ballpark?"

Barry answered for everybody. "The total headcount requests have come in at 467. I've given my team a challenge to trim that down to 425. I'd say you are in the ballpark. I foresee a similar situation next year and the year after that."

"Okay, now think about building scale into your operations. What if you didn't have to hire all those people? One way you can do that is to make your current employees work longer hours. That is not a tenable solution for the long-term, right?"

"Asking people to routinely work longer hours is absolutely the wrong approach. The hours are pretty long as it is. Our attrition has crept up lately. Nothing alarming, but I don't like the trend."

"So, what if you could maintain the same work hours and still be able to avoid growing your headcount without compromising quality, customer service, transactional cycle time, throughput, and all those wonderful metrics?"

"I'd give my right arm," said Barry, drily.

"Not your right arm, Barry!" begged Carl. "That's the arm you use to sign all those bonus checks!"

"Forget your right arm or even your left," said Jeff. "What if you could do that by merely clipping your nails?"

"Depends on how much this clipper costs," said Dan.

"Hold that thought, Dan, I'll come back to it" suggested Jeff. "Now, how many months did you spend launching your company, Barry?"

"It took myself and my team 24 months. That would be about 72 person-months, I'd say."

"Before you launched your company, were you a hot shot CEO of a fantastically growing company?" asked Jeff, knowing fully well what the answer would be.

"Not at all. I was a miserable director of a company whose growth curve had flattened out."

"Let's all look around this room," suggested Jeff. "In approximately three years, your company's growth curve will become almost flat unless you do something about it. Most of you, including you, Barry, will evolve–if evolve is the right word–into miserable directors and VPs of this company. Oh, you will make good money and a great living. But the excitement will be gone. Do you want to fix that? If so, what do you intend to do about it, hmmm?"

There was a clatter of nervous throats clearing and chairs scraping as people shifted uncomfortably. A poignant silence enveloped the room as they mulled over their options.

Only Barry gave tongue to their collective mood. In a soft voice, he said absentmindedly, "This looks like the famous yellow brick road to innovation."

Key Points

- Attention and think-time are the most important ingredients for creating growth and innovation.
- Companies spend too much time on low value, administrative activities. Busy work does not equal productive work.
- A good process management platform frees up employees from low value activities; it makes administration efficient.

9 Toto, We're Not in Kansas Anymore

The silence deepened as the management team digested Jeff's pronouncements. Of course, this was nothing they hadn't known. They wouldn't be holding down important positions if they weren't bright enough to read the writing on the wall. But it was the first time the situation was put so starkly to them. What made it even more inescapable was that Jeff had tantalized them with a glimpse of a solution.

That innovation drove the growth engine was a self-evident proposition. Jeff's development of the proposition pointed out that most companies lose the focus on growth and get sidetracked into making busy work. It was a problem that Jeff had challenged the team to attack.

"But we don't need huge innovation to grow," challenged Chuck Myers, the Head of PIQ. "We have a CGO, the Committee on Growth Opportunities. We have a healthy pipeline of growth ideas."

"That is a great step in the right direction," responded Jeff. "But I'd like to draw a distinction between innovation and growth ideas. You can grow your business through acquisitions, marketing plans, promotions, putting more feet on the street, and so on. All good companies lust after this type of growth, but it is not innovation. An innovative idea is a disruptive kicker to growth. Not all innovative ideas contribute to growth, but the possibility exists. Do you have the capacity to create an innovation pipeline?"

"I'd give my left leg to fix that," said Barry.

"Your golf would be off," quipped Marty, absently.

"No need to lose your left leg," assured Jeff. "I'm not talking about a major ERP implementation."

"Ah, those clipped nails!" said Carl.

"Did we file them or throw them away?" asked Dan, with heavy humor.

Guttural groans broke out.

"The key to continued innovation," said Jeff, "is to free up your minds from the routine, the administrative, the ordinary. You can't entirely avoid the routine, of course, nor should you. But think about it this way: avoiding costs by building scale is only one part of the equation. Pretty soon your competitors will be doing the same. Some of your competitors *are* actually doing this as we speak. What I am suggesting is that, unlike most of your competitors, you should invest in innovation."

"What you are saying," paraphrased Carl, "is that we take the savings you said are possible and use them to fund an innovation center, sort of an incubator."

"You could formalize it like that," agreed Jeff. "What if we find a way to eliminate an hour's worth of routine work per working day for each of your key employees? You and your employees could then redeploy your collective brain cycles to mull over innovation. For example, how many direct reports do you have Carl?"

"Eight."

"Eight plus you makes nine. How many of your indirect staff do you think can do a lot of leg work on innovative ideas? About 15, you say? To keep the math simple, let's say that there are 25 people in your department who could be excitedly pursuing innovation. One hour for every working day yields about 260 hours a year. 25 times 260 hours makes ... Dan?"

Dan was already typing away on his ever-present calculator.

"6,500 hours," he announced.

"That's just over three years."

"Three years and three months to be approximately exact," said Dan, in precise, clipped tones.

"Thank you, Dan. If you assume you need 72 person-months to launch your next innovative idea, how long till your next big spin-off at the assumed rate of time investment?"

Everyone looked at Dan as he busily clicked away. In a few moments he finished his calculations and began professorially, "If we assume ..."

"Cut to the chase, Dan," suggested Barry.

"Eh, of course," said Dan, smiling sheepishly. "It would take about one year and nine months. Building in some contingency, I'd say it would take two years."

"Now, Barry, you have twelve direct reports. This may sound like a stretch to you, but what if every one of your twelve departments did something similar? Let's be realistic though. Not all ideas will take fruit. I have seen one in ten, maybe one in five, that will blossom into a true growth opportunity."

"Let's not count on Midas and his folks—pun unintended—to come up with anything innovative. So, only eleven of us on Barry's team can be truly innovative," said Mark.

"Say what?" said Dan, rising to the bait. "Finance can be quite innovative. Have you forgotten SOX regulation? Basel? Changes to option expensing? The new FASB regulation on lease accounting? What about derivative instruments? Has securitization escaped your memory?"

"Oops! Sorry. I take back what I said. Finance can be very innovative. Too much at times. We have not forgotten 'creative accounting' or Enron."

"Dry up, you guys!" said Barry, laughing. "You can join the innovation teams, Dan, and cough up the cash to pay for our ventures."

"I'll need to see your projected ROI," said Dan, with gruff good humor.

"Regardless of how you look at it," said Jeff, "I believe this company can spin off another growth company within three years that may have the same chance of turning into a long-term viable business as its momma company."

"Why three years? I thought our calculations came up with two."

"You need at least one year to build capacity and to get your house in order before you'll get really efficient at investing time on new ideas. After implementing that first innovation spin off, your goal should be to establish a two-year cycle of innovation launches."

Dan, busily punching away on his calculator, said dreamily, "We'd have to build a good model on a spreadsheet to figure this out accurately, but assuming that the new spin-offs follow a similar growth curve, I think we would look at a consolidated growth rate of around 20%."

"Sounds incredible!" said Marty.

"Alright, so let's assume it is half that rate," suggested Jeff.

"Doesn't seem so hot then," observed Chuck.

Barry weighed in. "I think Jeff is setting up this growth through innovation to be accretive to our regular growth ideas," he said. "So, if we assume our regular growth rate in the long run stabilizes to around 12%, which isn't unreasonable given that it would be a little over the long run growth rate of S&P 500, our total growth rate would be pushing above 22%. Not bad at all, if you could make it sustainable."

"Your analysis is correct, Barry," said Jeff. Then he asked them a tantalizing question. "Now, the question is, which one of you on Barry's staff will be the General Manager of the first spin-off?"

There was a thoughtful silence for several minutes as they contemplated their expected compensation if they were to become the GM of a new spin-off. About half the members privately resolved to be that one individual. The rest were either skeptical or open to further exploration of the idea. Barry was contemplating how to foster some healthy internal competition.

"It's not easy to come up with innovation in our industry, you know," he began.

"Who says you have to stick to your own industry? Can you make forays into the fringes of your industry? What about a totally different one? In a decade, you could end up becoming a conglomerate. With none of the process-related integration problems that conglomerates face, of course."

"The only other concern I have," said Barry, scratching his chin, "is that innovation doesn't happen by spending time on it one hour a day. If an idea consumes you, there's nothing else you can think about. Everything else you do becomes utterly boring. You give up Monday night football, weekend barbecues, going to the theater, whatever."

Jeff addressed the objection. "Fair point," he said. "I can relate to that. I started on the business idea for my own company while I was still a corporate employee. I found that most things I did as an employee were utterly boring and ultimately, pointless. The backdrop of my burning entrepreneurial ideas forced me to be more efficient and focused at work. That allowed me the dual benefit of completing all my office work at the office and not bringing any of it home, and of staying excited and highly energetic at work. You can imagine how many meetings I pruned away, and how much more quickly I made decisions."

"That's an interesting angle," said Barry. "You put your finger on an itch that I always had, namely, that most employees were inefficient in what they did, which is why they worked way beyond forty hours a week. We are not really very productive, are we? We end up confusing quantity for quality."

"So, Jeff, tell us all about the magic elixir that'll make all this happen," broke in Marty.

"I bet it's that alphabet soup you mentioned earlier, Marty," said Mark.

"Yeah, that wham–bam thing," said Carl.

"New fads!" snorted Dan. "How many times have I heard this before? Client-server, object-oriented technology, death of the mainframe, Internet, eBusiness, and so on. All pipe dreams. No three-letter acronym ever amounted to anything."

"That's right. The bean counters only favor four-letter acronyms, like GAAP[39]," said Mark.

"You are making me out to be a snake-oil salesman," parried Jeff. "I can understand your skepticism. But are you open to discussing some new ideas? Or do you have a better alternative?"

"Oh, don't mind Dan," said Carl. "He believes in being close-minded. The product of all those years of closing his books regularly. I like to hear more."

"Come, come, you are being unfair to me," said Dan, twinkling at them over his glasses. "I like to hear more too. At the worst, I could use a good laugh."

---

[39] Generally Accepted Accounting Principles

"Good," said Jeff. "I always wanted to moonlight as a stand-up comic. Now, I'd like to explain some new ideas that have sophisticated technology components, but that have enormous implications for the way you run your business. I'd like to help connect the dots for you. Is it time for a quick break? I think it's important to maintain the momentum of thought and not get distracted. So, if you wouldn't mind, please don't leave the conference room to go check your emails or voice mails."

Saying this, Jeff promptly left the room to go use his cell phone to check on his voicemails.

* * *

When they reassembled, Jeff began, "I know that in the past we've had quite a few technologies touted as a panacea for everything, including world hunger. I have been in the thick of many of those, and they have had limited success. On the whole, I tend to agree with Dan that very few of those promises have been kept. I won't go into a diatribe on why those technologies did not work the way they were supposed to. However, a few trends have been underway in the past few years that reduce the risk of technology failure. The Internet boom gave us the testing ground for a few good ideas in technology, and a whole lot of bad business ideas."

"It gave new proof to the adage, *A fool and his money are soon parted*," said Dan, who, among all his friends, made the most return on his investment capital during the Internet boom by parking all his money in a checking account.

"What I can't figure out is how the fool and his money got together in the first place," countered Jeff. "Regardless, a few good things did transpire. For example, the complete infiltration of the Internet into every nook, if not yet into every cranny; a meeting of the minds between previously antagonistic technology companies on the subject of XML and Web Services; the creation of a tremendous amount of code in new languages;[40] and the delivery of open

---

[40] Such as Java, PHP, Perl, Python, C#, and other languages.

source web servers and application servers by Apache that saw widespread adoption.

"Never mind what all that means. The key thing to remember is that the mistakes that derailed earlier technologies won't be repeated by those who take the trouble to study history. I am sure we'll make some new mistakes, but my feeling is that we'll make them on the organizational front rather than the technological front."

Barry said, "Marty makes a big deal about SOA. He explained it to me several times, but I still don't get it. Not Marty's fault. I am technology-challenged."

"SOA is an important ingredient in the quest for process automation, but it is not the foundation of process management," clarified Jeff. "But let us quickly address it, since it came up. SOA stands for Service-Oriented Architecture. At its simplest it means building little services that do one thing well, and only that one thing. The smaller the service the better. An entire application can be built by 'threading' together a set of such services. In contrast to this approach, applications can be written as monolithic mountains of code. If you bought such a shrink-wrapped package that had, among other things, invoice creation functionality that you really liked and wanted to reuse in other applications, there would be no way to do it."

"Product vendors have a vested interest in putting into their products all the bells and whistles, and they are not interested in 'unbundling' their product. You have to use the whole thing or not at all," observed Marty.

"That's right. So, every application that you buy will have a user interface, some reporting functionality, its own database, and several modules of business functionality. I am sure you have seen the parts explosion diagrams that are displayed in automotive manuals. If you took each of your applications and exploded them into their functional parts, pretty soon you'd see a lot of common parts that have been used in numerous applications. Now, what if you could take one of the common parts, move it out of every application where it is duplicated, and redesign it as a 'service' that would be used by all the other applications?"

"All of my applications would get a bit skinnier?" hazarded Barry.

"I thought you said you were not tech-savvy! That's exactly right. We can't really do this for the commercial off-the-shelf applications. But apply that concept to applications that you'd build within your company. If you remove most of the duplicated code and allow your applications to talk to services that implemented common functionality, imagine how lean your systems would be."

"We would have some pretty slimmed down systems. I like slim better than fat. But where's the moolah in that?"

"The big benefit is that you'd be able to crank out applications or make changes to existing ones much faster."

"Fine, I like faster better than slower. Slow and steady wins the race, they said, but not if you are in the hundred meter dash, which is what we feel our business is in."

"So, where can we buy this SOA?" asked Mark.

"What does it cost, and how much can we really save?" asked Dan, predictably.

Jeff had a ready answer. "There is a store downtown, on the north side of fifth and twenty-third, called 'Whoa SOA!' Ask for B.P. Yum, and tell her I sent you. You'll get a nice discount on a few SOA packages. The ones from China, called 'chop soa,' are the best."

"Is it too much to hope that you are not kidding?"

"Unfortunately, there's nothing like an SOA package. You cannot buy it. Any more than you can buy GAAP. SOA is like a specification for designing applications. If you follow the rule book, everything will be mom and apple pie."

"So, let's break out the SOA cookbook and start coding away. I'll authorize pizza and diet coke. I believe that's the brain food de rigueur for the techies?" asked Barry, pretending to get up.

"I thought you'd never say that, Barry!" said Marty, sliding his chair back, clearly relieved.

"I have bad news for you," said Jeff somberly. "Implementing SOA as a first step towards creating a mature process management capability is absolutely the wrong thing to do."

"Why?" said Barry, settling back heavily into his chair.

"SOA is a technical issue. Would you buy a Ferrari if you could only drive it over muddy tracks?"

"Negative."

"Don't do this to me, Jeff!" pleaded Marty. "I have Barry where I want him."

"Don't panic, Marty. I'll do my best to convince Barry to give you SOA and much more besides. Have faith."

"So, what would you do first, if not this fabulous SOA?"

"Watch out! Here comes the rest of the alphabet soup," said Dan.

"Only one of the ingredients for now. Ladies and gentlemen, let me present to you BPM, or Business Process Management."

"Yummy!" said Dan, licking his lips. "Of should I say, B.P. Yum-Yum?"

Key Points

- Innovation causes disruptive growth, allowing a company to leap-frog over its competitors.
- Preoccupation with process inefficiencies and systemic inadequacies limit employees imagination, making them focus on 'what is' versus 'what is possible.'
- BPM allows a company to manage routine operations more efficiently, thus freeing up valuable mental resources to focus on growth and innovation.
- SOA makes rapid implementation of process improvements and process changes possible.
- BPM pioneer, Ismael Ghalimi, CEO of Intalio clarifies the roles of BPM and SOA: "BPM is SOA's killer application, while SOA is BPM's enabling infrastructure."

10 The Wizard at the End of the Road

"What will you have, sir?"

Jeff thought for a moment. "I'll have a vodka on the rocks with club soda, please."

"A slice of lemon, sir?"

"Lime, please."

Jeff took his drink and wandered away from the bar. He was immediately snagged by Dan, the CFO.

"I must tell you that you are the first consultant I've met who did not talk beyond a million dollars."

"Million dollar baby, that's what I am."

"So, you really feel that there is no need for a major investment to implement BPM and SOA?"

"Oh, you'll spend money all right," said Jeff, sipping his vodka with deep satisfaction. "But it is not like throwing money at a legacy migration initiative.[41] No matter how large the company, if you are spending more than a million dollars on any single initiative, then you are either doing something wrong or you are doing it the wrong way."

"I am not sure about that. Surely larger companies have larger problems?"

"That's rich, coming from a CFO! It doesn't matter how large the problem is. What can't stretch is the ability of one human mind to own a problem larger than a million dollars."

"Come now, I contest that. A lot of executives manage much larger budgets."

"There is a big difference between managing a budget and solving a critical problem. There are quite a few people who can easily handle a budget of several hundred million dollars. What they can't do is solve an active problem of that magnitude. Why do you think

---

[41] A project to replace an older legacy ERP system with another or with a newer technology, this almost always ends up costing several million dollars (and in some cases, even upwards of a hundred million dollars).

the failure rate of large projects is so high?"

"I agree that the failure rate is high, but the fact that it is not 100% disproves your theory. Shouldn't we focus on studying what makes some of the successful projects successful and duplicate that?"

"Let me throw a different perspective on this. Give me an example of one successful project over one million dollars."

"We implemented a CRM system that finally tallied up to almost one and one-half million."

"That's too approximate. Give me the exact cost."

"$1,468,300," said Dan without hesitation.

"Spoken like a true CFO! Now, tell me what benefit you obtained from it?"

"Better management of the sales force, better visibility into the sales pipeline. Lots of benefits."

"Remind me again what you do for a living. You are beginning to sound like a salesman from a product company. I am sure there were some of those benefits you mentioned. But what did that add to your bottom line? Can you attribute any increase in growth solely to it?"

"I am not sure about the growth, but we measured increased customer satisfaction."

"That's good. I assume therefore that your customers paid you more, or did not complain about your price increases? They placed more orders? They recommended your products and services to their friends and acquaintances?"

"They're definitely not going to pay more. As to the other metrics, we don't know that yet."

"But you do know you spent $1,468,300."

"Yes, that's easier to track. I am sure the benefits will show up within a couple of years on the CRM initiative."

"And you will be able to keep track of that?"

"I don't think we'd worry so much about tracking the benefits so exactly."

"That means that today you can't quantify the benefits of some multi-million dollar initiative you completed a few years ago."

"I have to agree with you on that," said Dan, reluctantly. He felt pinned to the corner. "But I see where you are going with that. How does spending less than a million dollars, say, $999,999, change the picture?"

"The issue with quantifying and tracking benefits still remains, of course. But your mistakes will be smaller, and you'll have the opportunity to learn more because you'll be executing a larger number of smaller projects. In fact, overall you'll make smaller mistakes because smaller projects allow you to deal with complexity. The project owner can handle that level of complexity better than he or she can handle a project one hundred times larger. An errant cost item of $100,000 is easier to spot and worry about when you are managing a million dollar project than when you are managing a hundred million dollar project."

Jeff steered Dan towards a window, and went through the ritual of lighting a pipe. Dan reminisced about other large projects he had overseen. All had the common theme that only the costs were coated on his bitter tongue, but no tangible financial benefits could be voiced.

"You are making my point," said Jeff, moving smoothly into a lull. "Incidentally, I wanted to provoke a thought with my arbitrary cap of one million dollars. It may be more or it may be less, but the point is that every company and every individual at every management level has a dollar amount that acts as the threshold between manageability and unmanageability. Furthermore, the identification and quantification of benefits is not exactly a science because projects are not executed in a controlled environment. Hence, it is impossible to attribute benefits causally to any one project with any degree of certainty."

Barry had quietly joined the conversation. He said, "But there is something called delegation."

"Yes, you can delegate authority. However you cannot delegate responsibility[42] and ownership, much as I hate to say it."

"You can and you can't. This is one of those subjects that gen-

---

[42] Byron Dorgan

erates an interesting, albeit purely academic, discussion."

"Let me un-academize it for you then, if you'll pardon that inventive word. You can delegate the day-to-day management of large projects, but then you are stuck with the problem of creating a measuring rod and administering it to the backsides of the delegatees. Bigger projects and bigger budgets create bigger egos. That creates an entirely different type of problem for you. So, let me recap the situation. You started off trying to solve a critical business problem. By scoping it to gigantic proportions, you acquire a measurement and incentive compensation problem. You then get saddled with a personnel management problem. Finally, because there are multiple organizational layers, you and your managers end up struggling with communication problems. You need all these additional problems? What's wrong with this picture?"

"We have no BPM, that's what is wrong with it," said Barry, wryly.

"I humbly submit that your diagnosis is wrong," said Jeff, completely oblivious to Barry's sarcastic tone.

"You turning down a clean segue into your evangelical BPM pitch? Remind me what you do for a living," suggested Dan.

"You'll regret saying that," answered Jeff. "The thing that's wrong with the picture is that you have no time for innovation."

"Aha, I knew innovation would sneak in somewhere."

"Let me get this straight," said Carl, who had been impatiently hovering at the fringes. "Some of the benefits of our IT projects may not be completely quantifiable and tangible. But they are nonetheless real. Why would you discount them?"

"Because you should! Just as you'd discount return on investment by risk. Let me ask you to force rank among the following: on the one hand I give you cost-out, increased productivity, decreased cycle time, and a host of similar benefits; on the other, I give you a new growth opportunity with an expected growth rate of 25%. Which would you pick?"

"The new business opportunity, of course."

"So, you did discount the other benefits in favor of new growth, did you not?"

Carl swirled his scotch on the rocks absently. The ice cubes beat a forlorn tinkling accompaniment. He made a valiant effort to salvage his position. "But, if I have no growth opportunities available, I can still go after the first set of benefits. I would be foolish not to."

"Agreed. However, you should first look about carefully to make sure you have no growth opportunities cooing and billing on the branches. The penchant of the human mind for creativity being what it is, you'll never run out of growth ideas, provided you have the time to indulge in the human penchant."

"So, you are saying that BPM and SOA, properly implemented, will free up the time for us to focus on the really important thing in life, namely growth through innovation," summarized Barry.

"Yes, but I'd add the following gravy. BPM and SOA, properly implemented, will also make a huge dent in inefficiencies, costly processes, and so on. This delivery of what we called intangible benefits is the secondary benefit, while the increased attention to innovation and growth is the primary benefit. Most companies get it backwards. They get caught up in implementing new technology or process improvements with the sole idea of reaping productivity and cost out, with no thought about the true purpose of business, namely growth. Therefore, when the productivity benefits do emerge, assuming the project is successful, the new capacity is filled up with non-growth activities and low-impact projects."

"So, our fundamental premise for initiating new projects is faulty?" asked Dan. He was still digesting this logic.

"Yes. Because, after every project you implemented, you filled up the newly freed up time with unnecessary activities. Pointless PowerPoint presentations, micro-analysis of financials, and worrying about productivity. If you did not have a well-tuned magnetic compass of innovation and growth, what else would you do with all that additional time? If you were pursuing growth and innovation, you would, to paraphrase Warren Buffett, be satisfied with being approximately right rather than being precisely irrelevant."[43]

"You don't pull any punches do you?"

"I think it makes a strange kind of sense," said Barry. "Let's imagine spinning off a new business that could grow at 25% AAGR[44] rather than worrying about consolidating a couple of systems for an unspecified 'feel good' benefit, or at best a minor financial benefit. Obviously, we wouldn't lose any sleep if the growth rate of the new business turns out to be 23% or 27%."

"There goes the approval for my server consolidation project request," grumbled Marty.

"I am not sure I entirely agree with you that a lot of our time is spent on useless activities," objected Barry. "Some of our time is wasted, I grant you. But not most of it."

"You could be right. Maybe your company is more efficient in how you administer your daily business. But I strongly recommend that you conduct a time analysis of your daily activities. For each activity, for each meeting, classify it as growth-oriented or non-growth. Don't contort the definition of the term 'growth-oriented' to allow the inclusion of questionable activities. Be ruthlessly honest with yourself. The best way to decide on how you want to classify a particular activity is to pretend you have a real double-digit growth opportunity awaiting your attention. I submit that whether you realize it or not, a potential growth opportunity is always waiting in the wings like a nervous bride. Ask yourself if you'd rather engage in the activity in question or work on your growth idea. The results may surprise you."

The group around Jeff was thoughtful. Indeed, several examples of wasteful activities were already springing up in their collective minds. Dan wondered about the excruciating financial analysis they conducted every Monday morning, debating the root causes of variation of a few basis points. Would a change of a few basis points matter much if they truly had a new idea ready to launch?

---

[43] "It is better to be approximately right than precisely wrong." Warren Buffett, 1993 Annual Report, Berkshire-Hathaway.
[44] Average Annual Growth Rate

Marty wondered if he'd worry about consolidating a few servers to reduce IT expenses by a couple of hundred thousand dollars a year if he had the opportunity to think about how to build functionality to handle a new acquisition or to launch a new product.

Carl wondered if he and his team would continue to hold painful debates on pipeline metrics, most of which did not change all that much on a weekly basis, if they were instead actively working on new marketing channels and new customer segments.

"You know, three years ago I went through a painful divorce," said Chuck, the Head of PIQ.[45] He had missed Jeff's earlier presentation at the company because of a customer meeting. He had been listening quietly to the discussion so far. "You know how it is when your marriage is going very smoothly. Your spouse could have a hundred faults, but love makes you indulgent, if not exactly blind, towards them. My wife used to kid me about not putting down the toilet lid, and I used to joke about her not putting enough salt in her cooking. I sat glued to the TV on Monday football nights, and she got bleary-eyed watching the cooking shows on Sunday. But once in a while we would glance at each other fondly.

"When things started to fall apart, for reasons we won't go into, all that changed. I mean, it may be okay to have an argument about politics or world hunger. But what we got into was laughable. The slightest thing irritated us both. We started bickering about the most inconsequential things. Looking back, it all looks so childish. I mean, is having the TV volume just a tad too loud sufficient cause for a screaming match? How silly was it of her to throw china around just because I forgot to bring the wine for a party at home? How idiotic of me to walk out and spend the night at a hotel just because she forgot to do the laundry?"

Carl put a hand on Chuck's shoulder. "Sorry to hear that."

Chuck, coming out of his reverie, looked around at them. "I am not being maudlin," he assured them. "That was all in the past. It's over and done with. But I could not help realizing that when a company's growth curve flattens out, it is like a marriage going sour

---

[45] Process Improvement and Quality

at worst, or becoming dull and boring at best. We end up arguing about the most inconsequential things. We drag ourselves reluctantly out of bed, knowing that we are going to bicker about a few more basis points, some small variation in cycle time, one lost sale, and a hundred other things that will not matter next quarter, problems to which no one will give a rat's ass a year from now."

Barry reached over and gently patted Jeff on the back. In his best avuncular tone, he said, "Jeff, son, you sure started something. The parallel between stagnant marriages and stagnant companies is uncomfortably appropriate. Have we finally come to the end of the yellow brick road to innovation?"

"We had better see a corporate marriage counselor then," said Dan. "Or should we say, the Wizard?"

They all turned towards Jeff and looked at him expectantly. He did not disappoint them. He straightened up, clicked his heels smartly, and said, "Dr. Jeffrey Sterllings, provider of Brilliant Panaceas for Marital Setbacks, at your Service! Outstanding Answers to your problems guaranteed."

Key Points

- The implicit goal of all companies is growth; focus on secondary objectives detracts attention from the true goal.
- Large projects create significant management overhead in delegation, ownership, communication, and accountability.
- Estimates of project benefits must be discounted by alternative growth opportunities, without which a true ROI does not emerge.
- An inordinate focus on trivial issues is symptomatic of a stagnant company.
- BPM and SOA do not require a major, ERP-like implementation (which is usually costly and time-consuming).
- BPM and SOA are not an all-or-nothing approach; they can be implemented incrementally, with benefits realized at every phase.
- BPM and SOA allow companies to be nimble, tackling a series of quick projects rather than large, monolithic, long-term projects.

11 Can LEAN Lean on BPM?

Marty Montrose woke up with a splitting headache. He groaned, propped himself up in bed, and moodily began to speculate on the meaning of life. After a few minutes he gave it up as too deep a subject to tackle before breakfast, and moved on to cogitate on more specific topics, such as why on earth he had to get up and go to the office. Seated at his breakfast table, he stared with undisguised hostility at his toasted organic wheat bagel. He took a knife and viciously spread cream cheese (lite) on it. After a few disconsolate bites, he took a sip of his decaffeinated hazelnut coffee, and immediately regretted it. He wondered how someone could have such a tortuously nasty mind as to invent such an abomination. Decaffeinated coffee! Now, that was a true oxymoron if ever there was one.

Things did not improve at the office. His hours were filled with excruciating episodes of crackers, diet cokes, slim-fast drinks, and more decaffeinated coffee. Lunch turned out to be a miserable event where he had to choose between various kinds of abominably healthy soups, appetizers and entrees. A fat-free protein bar, unaccountably renitent, chased down the gullet by a cup of decaffeinated tea, failed to provide relief as the afternoon rolled on. By the time the cows came home, the headache that had split his head in the morning went to work with renewed vengeance on the severed halves. Dinner time found Marty a confirmed misanthrope.

Jeffrey Sterllings watched his friend with amusement. They were seated at a fashionable downtown restaurant, the kind that frowns on bare arms on men, jeans on women, and tattoos on everyone. The lighting was subdued, conversation muted; soft strains of Vivaldi's *Spring* played a jocund counterpoint to the bleak wintry gusts outside, making a dull air bright and the bright air brighter.[46]

Jeff knew just what Marty needed. He turned to the waiter.

---

[46] Henry Wadsworth Longfellow, in *Evangeline*: "Many a glad good-morrow and jocund laugh from the young folk Made the bright air brighter..."

"Two vodkas on ice with club soda, slice of lime," he said.

"Two vodkas for me too," said Marty.

Jeff clicked his tongue. "Uh oh! Tell Uncle Jeffrey everything," he said in his best avuncular tone.

"Tell me," said Marty. "Why are health foods so disgusting?"

"They truly aren't. But relative to fat-laden foods, they are not so delectable. Taste is a complex sensation that has to do with flavor, texture, mouth-feel, and a characteristic called 'sticking to the ribs.' All of these culinary qualities are highly enhanced by fat. Without fat, flavors don't stand out, cooked foods end up dry, and digestion occurs rather quickly. The net result is a lack of a feeling of fullness and satisfaction."

"You prove my point. But is there no happy compromise?"

"If I really knew that, I might find a way to mint money. What brought on this sudden interest in healthy topics?"

"My doctor, who is a frustrated nutritionist. He's one of these new age types—strict vegetarian, no alcohol, no sugar, and a host of other no's. He's no fun. Now he's making my life miserable. He wants me to adopt his crazy life-style, otherwise he predicts an early demise for me. The way I see it, my options are either to have a great time and go out early, or be miserable and hungry for a long time."

Jeff sighed. "I agree that the idea of being lean is carried too far. You ever figure out where the term 'lean and mean' came from?"

"The product of some malevolent mind, no doubt."

"Au contraire my boy, my theory is that an obscure poet by the name of Shakespeare introduced it. In Julius Caesar, Act 1, Scene 2, good old Caesar says, 'Yond Cassius has a lean and hungry look, He thinks too much: such men are dangerous.' Methinks this is the origin of the phrase *lean and mean*."

"I can believe it. Julius was a wise man," said Marty, digging into his Caesar salad with enthusiasm. He had specifically asked the waiter to include real egg yolks in his salad. The piped music broke out into the slow second movement of Vivaldi's *Spring*.

"But sometimes lean is good, you know," replied Jeff.

"How do you mean?"

"Remember our conversation about Six Sigma?"

"How can I forget it? The debating points you gave me turned the situation around with Chuck, our Head of PIQ. Thanks to you, he came around to viewing BPM in a favorable light."

"Is Chuck into dieting?"

Marty stopped devouring his salad, astonished. "Chuck? Diet? Those two words cannot be used in the same sentence, unless it is to establish a negative correlation."

"I predict he'll start thinking about getting lean. Not himself, of course, but as it relates to process improvement and quality."

Marty paused in the act of transferring a spoonful of French onion soup from cup to lip. "Eh, come again?"

"Many of the organizations that adopted Six Sigma are coming to realize that the full DMAIC approach is like taking an elephant gun to a fly. They are looking at LEAN as a fast-track alternative."

"So, LEAN is the fly-swatter?" asked Marty, chomping into a skewer of satay.

"Exactly. Strictly speaking, lumping LEAN with Six Sigma is incorrect. LEAN by itself has nothing to do with the type of statistical analysis that Six Sigma became associated with."

"I'm not sure I understand completely."

"It must be your starved condition that is affecting your usual mental acuity."

"I'm working on the cure," mumbled Marty, happily slicing up a big chunk of steak tenderloin.

"LEAN is a methodology and a set of techniques to identify and eliminate waste in business processes."

"Sort of like my nutritionist's fads being a way to eliminate fat from the human frame," suggested Marty, ladling a humongous dollop of buttery mashed potatoes onto his plate. He paused, struck by a sudden thought. "No, scratch that," he said. "My nutritionist's fads are a surefire way to eliminate happiness from the human mind."

"True. Hopefully the LEAN methodology will stick to PIQ's ribs better than your nutritionist's diet sticks with you."

"I'm sure it will, especially if you are the one dishing it out," shot back Marty, recklessly pouring thick mushroom gravy onto his mashed potatoes. "Continue, O Leader of LEAN! You have my undivided attention."

Jeff looked at him doubtfully.

"Then listen carefully, O Disciple of DMAIC!" he began. "Imagine a group of employees getting together to fix a critical problem in their company. They are not really sure what the exact issue is. They can proceed in one of two ways. One, they can have a conversation, meandering back and forth, until they find the root cause of the problem. Then they can have some more conversation to try to find a solution."

The unmistakable strains of Vivaldi's *Summer* traipsed around the restaurant.

"Seems very inefficient to go about it like that. They should use a structured methodology, hopefully accompanied by a six-pack of the best," said Marty, helping himself to asparagus in cream sauce.

"Precisely. They can go with option two, a structured methodology, as you put it. DMAIC happens to be one such."

Marty groaned. "That's like starting to cook a seven-hour Jambalaya when you are starving. Not another one year project! I've had enough of those. Everyone in my company is tired of long DMAIC projects!"

"You just knocked the golf ball squarely for a 250-yard drive. But don't knock DMAIC. With careful management, DMAIC provides excellent rigor, forces you think rationally, and allows you to control the process once it's improved."

"I'm all for rational thinking," muttered Marty, sopping up the gravy with a buttered bread stick.

Jeff cast a quizzical eye at him. "If this gross violation of your nutritionist's advice is your example of rational thinking, then I'm a monkey's uncle."

"A brainy dude once said, *Foolishness every now and then, Makes for wise and sensible men,*" quoted Marty, slicing his tenderloin in time with the poem's meter.

"Have it your way," sighed Jeff, giving up a lost cause. "DMAIC turns out to be heavy machinery, not appropriate in all circumstances. Some companies found out that their employees were frustrated with the DMAIC approach, as in your case. Not because the methodology was bad, but because the employees were able to quickly hone in on the problem and suggest a solution. These employees did not see the value of an extended project when the solution was quite obvious to them. Why bother collecting reams of data, postulate arcane hypotheses, use sophisticated statistical techniques, and try to prove the point when the solution is staring you in the face?"

"Makes a lot of sense, of course. No need to employ formal methods when you know exactly what you want," declared Marty, waving away the dessert menu proffered by a solicitous waiter. "I'll have a key lime pie, truffle chocolates, a snifter of Courvoisier, and Turkish coffee," he ordered decisively.

"So, companies are in continual need of a structured methodology that would eliminate endless, profitless discussions, quickly zero in on problems and solutions, and document them in such a way that an improved solution is communicable and sustainable." Jeff paused.

Marty obliged him indulgently. "And what is this structured light-weight methodology, O Sultan of Slim?"

"Oh, come off it. You know it is LEAN."

"I'd never have guessed."

"LEAN is concerned with elimination of waste and those process steps that add no value."

"So, each process step is identified as wasteful or productive, value-added or non-value added, right?"

"The calories seem to be having an effect. You are regaining your mental acuity."

The haunting G-minor of Vivaldi's *Summer* gave way to the sobering F-major of *Autumn*'s allegro. Smugly, Marty continued, "So we could use a BPM platform to categorize our process steps and attach other pertinent data to facilitate analysis, right?"

"You are getting so sharp anyone who ran into you would be instantaneously julienned."

"I stole your thunder, did I?"

"By Zeus, I have more arsenal. LEAN doesn't merely ask that you make a superficial classification such as 'waste' or 'non-waste.' LEAN also dives into the various types of wasteful activities."

"The rationale being, I suppose, that it doesn't matter why an activity is productive, as long as it is productive, while it makes sense to examine why an activity might be wasteful."

"Something like that. LEAN deals with seven kinds of waste: transportation, waiting, overproduction, defects, inventory, motion, and extra processing."

"I can't remember all that!"

"You need a mnemonic hook. Imagine that your wallet is pretty lean because you have only 'TWO DIME' in it."

"I figured you'd have a cute memory aid like that tucked away. But," protested Marty, "TWO DIME is grammatically incorrect."

Jeff waved away the objection. "All the more reason you will remember it."

"This inventory of types of waste seems pretty comprehensive to me. But why is motion bad? I'd hate to be stuck to my desk all day. I like to move about."

"By 'motion' they mean any movement that does not add value to the activity you are supposed to perform. Do you know about the time and motion studies pioneered by Frank and Lillian Gilbreth, a husband and wife engineering-management team in the early 1900's? They had twelve kids. When they grew up, two of those kids wrote a hilarious book, 'Cheaper by the Dozen,'[47] that describes, among other things, how their parents conducted some of their time and motion studies. The Gilbreths pioneered the radical redesign of work motions. For example, in brick laying, they studied the motions that masons had been using without change for thousands of years. They redesigned these motions resulting in

---

[47] There is a Hollywood movie of the same name, ostensibly based on this book. However, Hollywood in its infinite wisdom, decided that the story of a football coach would be more within the grasp of the audience than time and motion engineering. Needless to say, the resemblance between the movie and the book starts and ends with the title.

the doubling of productivity. They also influenced the design of hospital operating rooms, and the placement of instruments and people around the surgery table to eliminate wasted motion."

"I'm sure I'll appreciate that if I ever lie under the meat cleaver. So there is no danger that a LEAN project will tie me down to my chair?"

"If pacing jostles the thoughts of a knowledge worker like yourself, feel free to wander about. Motion, in that instance, would be a value-added activity."

"You also classified inspection as a waste. I'm not sure I understand that. Isn't quality control important?"

"In many cases inspection is done because there is no confidence in the process, so someone needs to check up on the product. Not all inspection is bad, but you have to really examine it and see if you can remove the need for it by fixing something upstream. Imagine that the moment a defect is detected, the person who detects it calls attention to it. Depending on the type of process, that person, no matter how lowly in the hierarchy, is empowered to call a halt to the process. Assume that the defect is fixed right away, perhaps temporarily so that the process can resume, but an investigation is launched into the root causes of the defect, and a more permanent fix is eventually implemented. In this kind of environment, is downstream inspection really necessary?"

Marty sipped his brandy thoughtfully. Vivaldi's *adagio molto*, more familiarly known as *The Sleeping Drunkards*, invited everyone to sleep without a care.[48] "Seems to me that in this scenario inspection is done in 'real-time,' so to speak," he observed. "It is performed by the person who is closest to the part of the process that may result in a defect."

"Yes. That means a defect does not cause downstream defects. It does not cause a multi-stage rework. There would be no time wasted trying to identify the worker, the activity, or the original

---

[48] From the sonnet of the Autumn concerto of Antonio Vivaldi's Opus 8, No. 1-4, *The Four Seasons*, 1723: "The singing and the dancing die away, as cooling breezes fan the pleasant air, inviting all to sleep without a care."

conditions that caused the defect."

"The empowering of workers to call a halt when a defect is detected seems such an important concept that it ought to have a name."

"You are in luck. It is called *jidoka.*"

Marty looked at him with apprehension. "You are not going to make me learn Japanese, are you?"

"There is no need to learn Japanese, though I hope to persuade you to learn at least a few important words."

"I'm open to a bribe of Kobe beef. Fascinating as all this is, tell me more about the connection between LEAN and BPM."

"BPM provides the tools to support LEAN in many ways. Firstly, the modeling tools ensure that business processes are correctly classified into productive or wasteful steps; further, each wasteful step is classified into one of the seven kinds of waste. Another way to look at the process steps is to classify them as value-added or non-value added, as you rightly pointed out. You know from our earlier discussion that you can attach other kinds of information to the process steps. For example, you can specify the role or person performing the activity. You can identify what tools they use to perform the activity. In a manufacturing environment, the tools may be lathes, CNC machines, spray-painting machines, robots, and so on. In a services environment, the tools may be ERP systems, computer applications, or MS Excel spreadsheets."

"I can definitely see the value of attaching all this data to process steps. It would be very helpful for analysis."

"Right. You could answer questions such as, *Who is performing this wasteful activity?*"

"Or, *Which role is performing the most wasteful activity?*"

"Exactly. Or, *Which tools are being used for rework?*"

"What about, *What proportion of activities are value-added steps?*"

"Precisely. Moreover, a good BPM modeling tool allows you to document the processing time and idle time for each activity."

"So you'd know what proportion of the process' total idle time is coming from any particular type of waste."

"Bravo! All this analysis is only one part of the value you would derive from BPM. The second part of the benefit comes from the ability of a BPM platform to convert an improved business process into a detailed specification for implementing the improvement."

"This is deep. I'll need some assistance digesting it." Saying this, Marty snagged a passing waiter and ordered a refill of Courvoisier.

"There are two important ways that a BPM platform helps in implementation." Jeff positioned a chocolate truffle on the table. "This truffle," he said, "denotes the capture of business rules, roles, responsibilities, and other information about the new and improved process. It's the manual of standard operating procedures. BPM would be invaluable in organizing the information and presenting it for training. Nothing beats teaching employees about the new process in exactly the same format that was used to analyze and improve it."

Marty casually reached out, snatched the truffle, and popped it into his mouth. "I see that this information is for consumption by the business users. What's the other contribution of BPM?"

Jeff positioned another truffle out of Marty's reach. "The second way BPM helps in implementation is to take all the information gathered during analysis and modeling, and translate it into a model that is fairly easily consumable by the IT folks. These models are today almost exclusively based on XML.[49] The information may be presented as a pure XML document, or it may follow other formal and structured XML documents, such as UML,[50] BPEL,[51] and WSDL,[52] each of which have specific uses. A WSDL, for example, is a contract between a service and the 'outside' world, and is hence practically a necessity in enterprise integration."

Jeff turned away to signal for coffee. Marty quickly leaned over, grabbed the truffle, and popped it into his mouth. When Jeff turned back, he was met with an innocent expression on Marty's face. Jeff smiled when he saw that the table was sans truffle.

---

[49] Extensible Markup Language
[50] Unified Modeling Language
[51] Business Process Execution Language
[52] Web Services Description Language

"Looks like the technical specification went down very well with the IT community," he observed.

"Since we seem to be out of truffles, have we come to the end of the benefits of BPM in a LEAN environment?"

"Not quite. We haven't talked about process execution yet."

"There are more wrinkles on this BPM than on a dried prune. Perhaps I should order some cheese and fruit?"

"Suit yourself. The third wrinkle is the execution of the process itself. Some types of waste may be eliminated by automation. Some are eliminated by redesigning the process, with no need for automation. In all these cases, it pays to figure out how the waste is detectable. Is it directly detectable by the system, like inventory buildup? Or will a human detect it, and use the system to call a halt or log the defect? What if a worker misses detecting a defect? Can we design some redundant detection mechanisms?"

"What about idle times? How can those be monitored if the steps being performed are manual?"

"You may not be able to get very fine-grained in your ability to monitor idle times or wait times, but most manual steps are sandwiched between system touch points. If you can timestamp the system touch points, it would be easy to get some indication of nonproductive times."

"So the monitoring happens while the process is executing?"

"The *data* for monitoring is collected while the process is executing. It is not necessary for all of it to be displayed in real-time, or for the corrective actions to take place in real-time."

"You mean the need for real-time monitoring, feedback, and control is dependent on the criticality of the business process."

"That is correct. In addition to deciding how critical it is to keep on top of this monitoring data, you need to also figure out how to summarize the data and report on it. Some of the data or the reports may support business metrics. For example, call wait times and drop rates affect customer satisfaction."

"I take it this final piece is the Business Activity Monitoring."

"Quite right."

"If you don't mind, could you please summarize all this, Jeff? It seems we went all over the map on this topic."

"A little bit like your culinary excursion just now. Let me summarize by giving you the recipe. LEAN provides a structured, efficient way to identify problems and craft solutions. Some of the solutions may demand additional rigor that may be supplied by methodologies that are based on Six Sigma, such as DMAIC and DFSS.[53] Good BPM platforms support LEAN and all Six Sigma methodologies by enforcing the capture of information that will be utilized by business users, Quality experts, and Information Technology professionals. BPM ties together modeling, analysis, digitization, monitoring, and reporting. How's that?"

"I love it. Your summary has the flavor of a Unified Theory of something or the other."

"Nice way to put it. I'm going to adopt that expression. You know what comes next?"

"I can guess. One of your famous aphorisms?"

"I give you Sterllings' Theorem on Slimming: *LEAN takes the fat out of processes. BPM keeps it out.*"

"There is a corollary?"

"Of course! *Without BPM, lean processes crawl back to corpulence.*"

Marty was thoughtful. "We should alert Chuck that a new diet is in the offing," he said. "I am afraid he'll be devastated, though. He spent a lot of energy getting DMAIC accepted in the company."

"He can still splurge on the traditional approach if necessary." So saying, Jeff quoted:

> *Six Sigma is a useful methodology,*
> *No need for its premature elegy,*
> *A fast track option is LEAN,*
> *But if you fear you are turning mean,*
> *You can indulge in a DMAIC orgy.*

Marty leaned back, a beatific, contended expression on his face. He felt nothing but benevolence towards humankind. He was in full sympathy with the sentiment expressed by the lyrical *largo* of

---

[53] Design for Six Sigma: one of the Six Sigma methodologies

Vivaldi's *Winter* in F-minor: *To rest contentedly beside the hearth, while those outside are drenched by pouring rain.*

"I like that approach," he said, stretching lazily and yawning prodigiously. "The sun's shining," he declared, in defiance of actual fact. "The tenderloin is in the right place, keeping company with the pie, rubbing shoulders with the asparagus. They are all wallowing in the mashed potatoes and gravy. The brandy is playfully chasing the coffee. My nutritionist is nowhere in sight. Everything is copacetic."

Key Points

- While Six Sigma is a rigorous and intensely statistical approach to process improvement, LEAN offers a set of techniques to focus on wasteful activities and eliminate them.
- Waste in processes are classified in LEAN as transportation, waiting, overproduction, defects, inventory, motion, and extra processing.
- BPM's modeling tools offer excellent support to LEAN initiatives.
- BPM's model translation tools allow agility in implementing process improvements.
- BPM's information architecture ensures communication between the business, Six Sigma or Quality, and the IT functions.
- BPM's control framework keeps a 'lean' process 'lean.'

12 Windjamming With Control

Jeffrey Sterllings stood on the pier and gazed out at the bay. Khaki shorts exposed his knobbly knees, a sailor's jersey protected his middle, and a white cap adorned his head. Chuck, standing to his left, was enclosed in a thick jacket and scarf. He had a pathological intolerance to wind and cold. Whiffs of cool breeze skipped across the water, whipped around Jeff's exposed knees, and danced a frigid hornpipe on Chuck's ears. Jeff, glancing at Chuck enviously, wondered if he should have dressed more warmly. Chuck wondered if he should have brought his earmuffs along, though they would have looked ridiculous on him at this time of the year.

Only Barry seemed completely in his element. He was dressed as if here were just on the way to the local pub: faded blue jeans, white turtleneck t-shirt, a casual cap, a light windcheater, and walking sneakers. He sniffed the air appreciatively, and sauntered over to Jeff and Chuck.

"Seems to be a promising day for sailing," he pronounced. "Just the right level of breeze—look at those puffs of wind on the breakers."

"How deep is the water here?" asked Chuck, nervously. He also had a pathological intolerance to water outside his bathtub.

"Relax. No more than three fathoms around here. Out on the sound it descends down to about fifteen fathoms."

Chuck's nervousness increased visibly. His aversion to water was compounded by the fact that he could not swim.

"Relax, mate!" put in Jeff, kindly. "You can wear a life jacket." He pointed to a heap of life jackets piled on the pier, waiting to be picked up by the boaters.

Chuck looked at them dubiously, shifting his glance from them to his own ample middle.

It was the annual outing for the company's top management, styled with a different theme each year. This time Barry, being a sailing enthusiast, had prevailed on them to give his hobby a go.

His colleagues, teamed up in groups of two or three, were getting into the sailing boats. Each boat had either an experienced sailor or a sailing guide hired from the local sailing club. Barry, with his considerable experience in all things nautical, appointed himself the captain of his boat. Chuck and Jeff were chosen to accompany him, Jeff being invited as an honorary 'friend of the company.'

Aboard the little sloop, Chuck valiantly struggled into a large life jacket as Barry gave them instructions.

"Rules of safety," he pronounced in a commanding tone. "Be seated as much as possible, keep your life jackets on, watch out for the swinging boom, and keep a hand on the lines or the rails if and when you do move about…"

Jeff, listening intently, pulled out his pipe.

Barry continued, "…and no smoking. Fire and sails don't mix. There's an icebox in the cabin with sodas and beer."

"I thought it was alcohol and water that don't mix," said Jeff.

"They don't," replied Barry, with a cunning look. "That's why, do take care to put the beer into you and not into the sea. I understand both of you have zero experience in sailing? Never mind. I'll explain the ropes as we go along. I'll be the skipper, and when I bark out an order, your job is to repeat it and go 'aye, aye.' Understood?"

"Aye, aye, skipper," chorused Jeff and Chuck.

"Excellent! That's the idea. Now, Jeff, you be the helmsman, okay? Chuck, you be the…," Barry paused and looked at Chuck uncertainly.

Chuck seized the opportunity. "How about I be the marine administrative officer on land?"

"I have no problem with that. Feel free to head back to shore," said Barry, with a twinkle in his eye.

Chuck stood up eagerly, but his elation turned to dismay when he realized that the boat was several yards away from the pier: they had gently eased away when Barry was giving them instructions.

"Never mind, Chuck," said Barry, kindly. "We'll find something for you to do. Don't worry, you will be perfectly safe. If nothing else, we'll send you below deck to double as ballast."

Barry stepped over to the small outboard motor, started it, and gently guided the boat out into the harbor.

Jeff looked at the motor askance. "We use an outboard motor to go sailing," he observed. "Makes perfect sense of course."

"Only to go out into the bay," clarified Barry. "I'll have the sails up in a minute or so."

"If we are becalmed, we could use the motor, yes?" asked Chuck, desperately looking for reassurance.

"Sure. Only if you want to be tarred, feathered, and ridden out of town on a rotting mast by a mob of disgruntled sailors."

Within a few minutes Barry turned off the motor and went through the routine of putting up the sails. He explained what he was doing as he went along, breaking down the steps into the simplest atoms of action for the benefit of Jeff and Chuck. After they had finished hoisting up the jib and mainsail, Barry ordered Jeff to take the helm.

"Aye, aye, captain," replied Jeff, smartly. He looked around vaguely for a few moments, cleared his throat, and asked, "Eh, skipper, where–and what–is the helm, and where do you want me to take it?"

Barry displayed monumental patience and took a deep breath.

"You see that long rod on a pivot?" he pointed out. "That's the tiller, also called the helm. It is connected to the rudder. Together, they form the steering mechanism for the boat."

"I got it. I suppose I swivel it left or right to go left or right?"

"Not quite. You swivel it left or right to go starboard or port"

"I see. I have only one more question for now."

"What's that?"

"Which is port and which is starboard?"

* * *

Soon, they were well under way, the susurrus of the water cleaving past the bow punctuated by an occasional billowing crack of the sails. The boats of their colleagues languidly crisscrossed ahead and astern, as they tacked and jibed to ride the capricious wind.

"See those strips of ribbons stuck to the middle of the sails?" said Barry. "They are called telltales. They help you steer the boat. Your job is to keep them fluttering away in as straight a line as you can make it; don't let them stall, hang limp, or flutter about listlessly. If they do, that would mean there is no wind flow along the surface of the sail, which would cause us to lose power. You'll have to adjust the rudder to manage that. Keep a light but firm hand on the tiller."

Barry turned to Chuck.

"I'll be the tactician," he said, "so I'll be on the lookout for bursts of wind skimming across the waves so we can prepare to change direction. You'll help me trim the sails and assist me in tacking and jibing. I'll explain carefully what all that means as we go along. Now, let's do an exercise in tacking, alright? Helmsman, thirty degrees to starboard."

"Thirty degrees to starboard, aye, aye, skipper," yelled out Jeff, and smartly shifted the tiller thirty degrees to the right. The boat promptly headed to port.

"The other way, you landlubber!"

Within the next hour, Jeff and Chuck became nodding acquaintances with the main points of sailing, Chuck doing more nodding than acquainting. Jeff, his neck craned upwards, kept his eyes glued to the telltales; he began to acquire a feel for the pull of the rudder and the undulating oscillations of the boat. He quickly mastered the art of making micro-adjustments to the tiller to keep the boat moving at optimum speed. When the wind changed, Barry called out the tacking maneuvers. Chuck and Barry changed positions as they shifted the sails. They all took care to keep out of the way of the swinging boom, clued, no doubt, by Barry calling out "Duck! Duck!" On these occasions, Jeff and Chuck answered, "Quack, quack, skipper."

Chuck, his fears laid to temporary rest, began to entertain them by thinking up the names of various brands of 'port wine,' using the word as a homonym for the left of the boat. For example:

Barry, in rough baritone: "Hard a port!"

Jeff, answering in tenor: "Hard a port, aye, aye, captain!"

Chuck, simulating a gruff bass worthy of Long John Silver: "Hard a Dow Vintage, aye, aye, skipper!"

Barry: "Forty five degrees to port!"

Jeff: "Forty five degrees to port, aye, aye, captain!"

Chuck: "Forty five degrees to Royal Oporto White, aye, aye skipper!"

Barry challenged Chuck to come up with the name of a port wine every time he used the word 'port' in a nautical command, with the proviso that no brand name was to be repeated. Needless to say, Barry engaged in many unnecessary maneuvers just for the privilege of tacking to port. It also went without saying that Chuck made up quite a few fictitious brand names with no one the wiser. By the time they sailed back to the clubhouse pier a few hours later, Chuck was declared the winner. Barry bought him a Fonseca '97 Vintage Port from the club cellars. Chuck, eschewing the convention of imbibing port as a post-prandial potation, promptly opened it and passed it around to the rest of his colleagues as they trickled into the club lounge to relax until dinnertime.

"What did you think of the sailing experience today, Jeff?" asked Barry.

"Very eye opening. I really enjoyed it. I have acquired a deep and abiding appreciation for the ancient mariners. It seems incredible that they embarked on ocean voyages with nothing but the stars and their indomitable courage to guide them."

"You have a way of finding an analogy between BPM and any given situation. I challenge you to find one between sailing and BPM."

"You are in a betting mood today! That's a dangerous challenge to give to an evangelist. Everything looks like a nail to my BPM hammer."

"How about we wager a case of your favorite pipe tobacco?"

"You are on!" said Jeff, his eyes gleaming.

"This I have to see," said Chuck. He shepherded together Marty, Dan, Carl, and a few other colleagues. "Come on guys! Barry has challenged Jeff to come up with a way to use sailing as an analogy for BPM."

They replenished their drinks and arranged themselves on the sofas and chairs in the lounge. Jeff took a sip of his Fonseca port, cleared his throat, and began, "This is my first time sailing ever. I am impressed how much there is to it."

"It was my first time too," said Carl. "I thought that sailors merely hoisted sail and went wherever the wind took them. Or if they wanted to head in a particular direction, I thought they just waited until the wind was blowing their way before raising sail."

"Just as some managers think that all they have to do is buy an ERP system off the shelf and they are good to go," observed Jeff, dryly.

"Hopefully you learned that with careful tacking you can go pretty much anywhere you want," said Barry.

"Another interesting thing I noticed was how quickly we were able change direction," continued Jeff. "Barry had this uncanny ability to spot a puff of wind out on the water. He always had us execute the maneuvers to time the moment the gust of wind reached the sails."

Barry waved a self-effacing flipper. "Nothing uncanny about it. Most sailors who have some salt rubbed into their skin know how to do that. In fact, the position of tactician is very critical. A tactician knows how to take maximum advantage of changes in wind, current, and tides, and to keep a safe course."

"The two critical capabilities that we can take from sailing and apply to your company–any business, in fact–are the ability to detect changes in the environment, the ability to change direction quickly, and the ability to keep the business stable," observed Jeff.

"Those are three capabilities," corrected Dan.

"Thanks, Dan. I miscounted. Blame it on this excellent port wine."

"I'm afraid to ask, but how do you relate those three key abilities to BPM, and how would you apply them to a business?"

"You are right to be afraid. You are going to lose the bet, Barry! Those three capabilities as they apply to sailing are a perfect match with the capabilities of BPM. Business Activity Monitoring, or 'BAM' for short, is the ability to monitor what is happening in your business. For BAM to be truly effective, the metrics that you track should be clearly tied to business measures, the data behind them should be reliable, and the metrics should be fairly current. All metrics need not be available in real-time, but they need to be as close to the criticality of the business situation as possible."

"BAM is going to monitor the business from a transactional standpoint. How will that help us detect trends? Don't you think your claim is a bit of a stretch?"

"I agree with you that when it comes to detecting trends and predicting business events, BAM cannot act in isolation. I'd be the first to disabuse anyone of that idea. By trends, I don't necessarily mean the large strategic trends. We can think about customer demand, inventory buildup, customer inquiries, and other tactical measures and indicators of processes going out of control."

Barry became animated. "You just used the two magic words, 'process' and 'control.' Chuck and I were discussing this the other day. I was asking him how we could do a better job with the control phase of our process improvement projects."

"That's right," said Chuck. "We seem to start projects with a fanfare, but six months after they are done, we never revisit the processes periodically to see if they are still in control."

"Not many companies are good with managing the control phase of PIQ," said Jeff. "After all, the glamour is in starting and finishing, but not in maintaining. This is analogous to leaving on a sea voyage with a band playing and champagne popping, or the equally fanfare-filled arrival, while the days at sea settle down into a humdrum existence. Similarly, when you implement an improved process using DMAIC, you do establish upper and lower control limits for it. But rarely do companies establish a good process—we should really call it a *meta*process—for monitoring the business process or for keeping it under control. There is no thrill in doing so."

"I can see how BPM would help in keeping a process under control," said Barry, "but you haven't earned your case of tobacco yet."

"Ah, the connection to sailing! I'll weave that in. When the new to-be process is modeled, the control points should also be defined and captured as part of the process documentation. Various process metrics should also be defined. For example, you may be interested in the cycle time between process steps numbered 23 and 49. A good BPM platform would allow you to tag those process steps as the start and end of a named cycle."

"So, the specification of these controls and cycle metrics would be made available to the IT development team, allowing them to build the necessary digitized controls," said Marty.

"Exactly. The final dot to connect is the reporting of those control points and business metrics through the BAM dashboard. When Barry told me to keep an eye on those little fluttering ribbons on the sail to make sure we don't stall, I realized that they were similar to business metrics. I also realized that very small adjustments in the tiller were enough to keep the sails fully fluffed—that may not be the correct nautical term—but you get my drift."

"I hate to help you win your bet, but I'm guessing that the tacking and jibing we did have something to do with business agility."

"Thanks, Barry. You almost signed the check paying for my case of pipe tobacco. BPM in fact does have the machinery to help you change the direction of the business quickly."

"I'm not signing any checks until you clarify that."

"Gladly. Long ago in a far off time, corporate managers had to ask their MIS departments to churn out some numbers, which typically took anywhere between a few hours to a day or two. The managers looked at the results, and then thought up a what-if scenario. They sent the report back to the MIS department and asked them to redo the report with a few changed assumptions. Again, there was a turnaround delay. And so it went."

"Then came the magic of spreadsheets!" said Dan.

"I knew you'd like that part! VisiCalc[54] made an appearance, and the world was never the same again. Today, you'd fire up your spreadsheet and play with it to your heart's content. The IT department is no more called on to mediate between the spreadsheet user and the spreadsheet application."

---

[54] Developed by Dan Bricklin in 1979.

"I knew it," said Marty, gloomily. "BPM is like that spreadsheet, but for more complex applications. There goes my job!"

"Unfortunately, that's a good analogy. Fortunately for IT, I don't believe that the nirvanic scenario of eliminating an entire IT department will happen within the next decade. After that, I have no clue what might happen. I don't care and neither should you."

Marty perked up. "Great, I get to keep my job!"

"For now," grunted Barry.

"Technology is too complicated to be replaced completely by automation. BPM merely, though 'merely' is understating it, makes IT's job more interesting."

"Business is too complicated for technology to replace people," observed Carl.

"You are chanting my mantra, Carl," agreed Jeff. "Remember our discussion on innovation? The main point I made at that time was that you can use BPM to become very efficient, but the bigger benefits come about because you free up your employees from the mundane and get them excited about innovation and growth."

Barry was thoughtful. "How would you recommend we keep a firmer hand on our corporate rudder?"

Jeff held up a finger. "First, as part of your requirements specification on every project, have your business analysts ask themselves, 'How will we know when this process, subprocess, or process step goes out of control?' Have them define the control points, the process spec limits, and other metrics for each process or part of the process thereof. Have them find out who needs to know if and when the process goes out of control. Have them figure out who needs to be kept informed of the process staying in control. These define the two kinds of notifications."

Chuck commandeered a white cloth napkin and started to take notes on it.

"What exactly is the distinction between those last two kinds of notifications?" asked Dan.

"Normally, when processes are in control, some people need to know that fact, mostly because a process in control triggers other processes. Sometimes, it's not humans who need to know, but perhaps some IT applications need to be notified so they can start executing. That's one kind of notification, or 'message,' as it is called in IT when it applies to inter-systems communication. Then we have the other kind of notifications—the exceptions, the fire alarms, and the tearing sounds of a business coming apart at the seams. Internal auditors, senior management, escalation specialists, and similar personnel need to be alerted."

"I agree. I don't necessarily want to know that things are going just fine, but I do want to know PDQ when things are blowing up," confirmed Barry.

Jeff's middle finger joined his first. "The second thing you do is to ensure that your IT developers program those control points into the application. The information about who needs to know the two kinds of notifications must be programmed into the systems. In some cases, the program calls for an email alert to be sent out, or a number in large red font to show up on a dashboard; in other cases, a message needs to go out to another IT application."

Marty snagged a napkin and scribbled furiously. He stole a glance at Chuck's napkin to copy Jeff's first point.

Jeff's ring finger stood up at attention. "The third thing to do is to ensure that the metrics captured by the control points are stored in a business intelligence solution."

"You mean the data warehouse?"[55] asked Marty, making a thorough calligraphical mess on his napkin.

"Yes, though it could be a data mart,"[56] elaborated Jeff. "You'd do that to ensure future reporting, analysis of trends, generating analytic views, and so on."

A waiter approached, carrying two notepads. Clearing his throat nervously, he extended them towards Chuck and Jeff.

"If you two gentlemen wouldn't mind using these…" he began.

---

[55] A specialized database that houses aggregate or summary data for the purpose of reporting.

[56] A subset of a larger data warehouse, a data mart typically contains data limited to a function (such as finance, sales, marketing, etc.) or to the data from a particular application (such as a CRM system).

The two gentlemen waved him away.

"Put the two napkins on the tab," ordered Chuck.

The waiter departed, but not without deftly relieving their table of the remaining napkins.

Jeff's pinkie rose up to join its comrades. "The fourth, the final, but the most important thing to do, is to ensure that senior management always—ALWAYS—reviews control metrics of completed projects at their regular project review meetings."

Barry looked around for a napkin to memorialize this nugget of wisdom. He was about to use the back of Carl's t-shirt, but Chuck intervened.

"It's okay, boss," reassured Chuck. "I got it."

"Good," said Barry. "Anyway, Chuck, that's your job. From now on, make sure you always have your folks report on control metrics. Tell them that until they report out on the metrics from their past process improvement projects, they won't get their new projects approved."

"So let me recap for my own benefit," interjected Marty. "Jeff, you mentioned three capabilities. The first was the ability to detect change. BAM does that, much as Barry the Blackbeard detects changes in wind and wave with his sharp eyes. The second was the ability to change direction quickly, like the tacking and jibing. BPM enables business agility by giving business users more control over business rules and process flows, and to make a limited—and carefully defined—set of changes without having to seek help from IT. The third capability was to keep the boat stable, without swinging wildly all over the ocean. The helmsman keeps a firm hand on the rudder. In a BPM-mature company, all business processes have well-specified control points in their documentation. They also have a mechanism, such as project reviews, to keep them under constant scrutiny."

"Very good summary, Marty. I'll split my tobacco with you. By the way, did I win my barrel of tobacco yet?" queried Jeff.

"All right, I concede," said Barry, graciously. "In fact, you won four cases, one for each tobacco-stained finger you brought up."

"How come you are not so benevolent with our bonus, boss?"

asked Marty.

"I wasn't being generous with the company's money, Marty" re-assured Barry, soothingly. "You and Chuck are each paying for a case out of your own pockets, since the company has to pay for those two napkins you clowns ruined."

Chuck cast a slow, mournful glance at the assembled company. Morosely shaking his head, he declared, "I knew I shouldn't have boarded Blackbeard's barmy boat."

Key Points

- Detecting changes in the business environment, changing direction quickly, and keeping the business stable are three critical capabilities that BPM provides.
- Business activity monitoring, a key component of BPM, allows a company to detect changes in its operational processes and its customer-facing processes.
- Key process characteristics can be compared to the tolerance limits set by process improvement efforts.
- Identifying failure points and out-of-control situations should be part of process analysis.
- Control points should be designed into the IT solution.
- Process dashboards may be integrated into an existing business intelligence (BI) solution, or used as the basis for a new BI capability.
- Make the review of process control metrics part of the regular operating mechanism of the business.

13 The Taming of the Whip

Dan Manning, the CFO, looked at the thin-lipped man sitting across from him. His brow formed a mountain ridge. His brain slowly thawed from the shock he had received. He gingerly tapped the folder lying on the table, with the air of a man patting a hooded cobra on its head.

"Is this for real?" he asked, his voice shaky.

"You think I would kid about something like this?"

"I guess not," said Dan reluctantly. "You auditor types have no imagination and no sense of humor."

"I'll take that as a compliment. The question now is, what are you going to do about it?"

"You have to give me some time to digest this."

The auditor took off his round glasses and carefully polished them with a white handkerchief that he fished out of his pocket, and then carefully adjusted them on this long roman nose. He teased an errant strand of hair back into place on his meticulously cropped head, and brushed away an imaginary speck of lint from his shoulder.

"Take all the time you need," he said. "Only, make sure you get them all addressed within a month."

Dan exploded out of his chair. "You must be out of your mind! How do you suggest I solve all these in one month?"

"That's your problem, not mine. I merely report the issues. I follow the guidelines of the Board of Directors."

"You are enjoying this, aren't you?"

The auditor uncoiled slowly from his chair. And uncoiled. He was tall, spindly, and willowy. A prominent Adam's apple bobbed up and down when he spoke. He seemed to be put together with left over angles and sharp corners.

"I enjoy my job, yes. I derive no particular satisfaction in causing headaches for others. I'm sure you agree the issues listed in these files must be fixed. In the end, this will only make us a better and stronger company." The auditor gathered up his briefcase and headed towards the door.

"Spare me the cant," said Dan, flipping a hand wearily. "Of course I know that. I don't debate that these issues must be fixed. But there is no way on earth that I can solve them all in one month."

The auditor paused, his hand on the door knob. "Oh, I don't expect you to actually solve the problems in one month. The guide-line from the Board is that the management gets one month to come up with a feasible plan to solve the problems."

"Who decides the plan is feasible?"

A slow smile spread out on the auditor's lips. "The Board does," he said. "With my input. Have a nice weekend!" The auditor stepped out into the corridor.

The door swung back and clicked shut. Dan sat back heavily in his chair. He stared at the thick folder with dismay. "One lovely weekend coming up, right on schedule," he muttered.

***

"I think I should have been informed about this. Why didn't you give me a chance to study the situation, run my own audit, and fix the issues?"

"Because," replied Barry, patiently, "that would be like asking the fox to mind the hen coop. Now, now, don't get mad! No one's accusing you of being biased or unethical, but you know we can't allow even a hint of conflict-of-interest situations. That's why we have an independent audit department."

"I know. I just can't help feeling the way I do."

"If it's any consolation to you, some of these audits happen without my involvement either. I wouldn't want any opportunity to prejudice or influence the outcome. If anything blows up, I don't want even the slightest suspicion floated around that I influenced or hindered the investigation."

"I guess that's a positive way of looking at the situation," said Dan, grudgingly.

"Anyway, what brought this on? Give me the details."

"Two hundred seventy six," said Dan, plunking himself into a chair.

"Is that the answer to world hunger? Unified superstring theory? Average annual income of the planet? Life and meaning in the universe? Throw me a bone here."

"That's the number of violations to controllership and compliance in our business."

"I see. Is there any substance behind those, or are they simple examples of someone forgetting to type in the exception waiver code on a deal?"

"There are a few simple examples of the kind you mention, but they are not isolated examples. They are indicative of much deeper, systemic problems that point to a lack of data integrity."

"Regulatory problems? Sarbanes-Oxley?[57] FASB?"[58]

"I will walk you through the various folders in a minute, but regulatory issues are only a subset, though by far the most serious subset, of all the issues. I don't think any of these items will be a surprise to you..."

"I agree," interrupted Barry. "That's why I hired you. We knew we had problems, or if we did not, we knew our lack of internal controls would create problems in the future."

"What truly surprised me was the ease with which our internal auditor unearthed them."

"Again, if it's any consolation to you, I am sure his investigation wasn't easy or quick. He started on his audit six months ago. By the way, the more you get to know Nathan the more you'll respect him. He's is good at his job because he's as persistent as an incurable rash."

Nathan Edwards was the internal auditor who reported to none other than Rex Skiller, the Chairman of the Board, and not to Barry, who was the CEO and President.

Dan was still uncomfortable. "I have a nagging feeling I wasted

---

[57] The Sarbanes-Oxley Act of 2002
[58] Financial Accounting Standards Board

some of my time and all the time of three of my staff members who were doing a similar internal audit," he burst out. "If Nathan had informed us, we could have pooled our resources or got it done faster."

"I think the parallel efforts will be illuminating precisely because they are not coordinated."

"Huh? You lost me on that one. I thought the priority was to discover control problems and fix them, not worry about who finds out what."

"The priority, from an external perspective, is to actually fix and prevent such violations. However, from an internal perspective, it is important to figure out how good our internal procedures and organization are in detecting such violations."

"Check the checks and the checkers, eh?"

"Exactly. For example, if your staff came up with a small subset of what Nathan kicks out of the weeds, then you need to train your staff to be better detectives. Or your staff may compile a much more exhaustive list. Then we would have to figure out what made Nathan and his team miss those items."

Dan turned thoughtful. "Someone could be uncooperative or misleading. The consequences could be serious."

"Or Nathan must be given a freer hand to dig even deeper and more thoroughly."

"I do agree that independent investigations are not such a bad idea. Did you put this strategy together yourself?"

"Rex and I discussed it. Remember, independent audits are a requirement of the Sarbanes-Oxley Act. We decided to expand the scope of the audit beyond financial controls, by including areas of enterprise risk. You could say we share the responsibility for masterminding the specifics."

"No wonder Ami keeps calling you 'boss.' This has all the trappings of running a spy network. Verify sources, check against multiple reports, look for inconsistencies. All that cloak-and-dagger stuff."

Barry chuckled appreciatively. "Very perceptive, Dan! Rex used to be an Assistant Director of the CIA in a prior life."

"Ah! Say no more."

"Come, let's move over to the sofa and relax for a bit. Let me make you an espresso. You can read out to me the juicier bits and pieces from Nathan's report."

Dan winced. Ever since someone thoughtlessly gave Barry an espresso machine as a Christmas gift, Barry inflicted his espressos on every visitor. This would not have been such a bad thing were it not for the fact that Dan couldn't stand espressos. He yearned for a regular coffee with all the trimmings.

While the deplorable machine hissed and gurgled sinisterly, Dan extracted several sets of stapled sheets from an accordion folder, and spread them about on the floor and on the table in front of the sofa.

"I am now reading from the summary report. Nathan classified his findings into several categories that are rather unconventional, yet insightful. The broad internal audit categories are 'Process Audit,' 'Product Audit,' and 'Organizational Audit.' The rest of the files are the details for each of these categories."

Barry nodded thoughtfully. "The categories seem to cover the how, the what, and the who."

"Yes, you might put it like that. So, under 'Organizational Audit,' he asks and answers the question, 'Are the right people doing whatever they are supposed to be doing?' For example, here is a violation: 'Engineering manager approves selection of suppliers and also pays their invoices.' That occurred in product engineering."

"Clearly, we can't have that," said Barry. "I know the engineering manager in question. He's a good guy, but we shouldn't tolerate a practice where someone might accuse him of paying his own brother-in-law."

"Here's another: 'Software developers are also testing the final application.' I thought they were supposed to do that."

"Absolutely not. Testing should be done by an independent quality assurance team. Marty is aware of that one. In fact, he is working with HR to create a small, independent testing team."

"Good," said Dan, clearly pleased that some of the items in the report were already being addressed. "Many of the violations refer to improper documentation. All these are classified under 'Product Audit Violation,' which is surprising until you realize that by the word 'product' Nathan means any artifact produced by business processes."

Barry handed Dan a cup of espresso. "Is he claiming that the documentation is missing or that it is inadequate?"

"Both. And more. For example, too much documentation, meaning multiple copies that are all different versions of the same document. You know how much chaos that would cause."

"I get the drift," said Barry, taking a satisfying sip of his brew. "You know how many times I have torn my hair out in staff meetings when some important report is outdated. How about those times when we have to honor a low-margin contract because field sales used an old price sheet?"

Dan, unable to put off the inevitable any longer, took a cautious sip of his java. A spasm of misery flitted across his face, but he quickly arranged his features into a semblance of nonchalance. He quietly vowed to unearth the espresso gift-giver's identity and punish the culprit by sending his kids a drum set.

"Let me show you how all the files are organized," he said, pointing to the stacks spread out about them. Each group of neatly stapled stack of papers covered a major area of controllership.

"Here," began Dan, tapping on one of the stacks, "is a list of violations in section 404 of SOX legislation." Dan moved on to the other stapled sheets. "This one is for violations in internal controls for operations; this one deals with our shortcomings in reporting that go beyond the financial statements; and this yellow folder describes our lack of controls over our technology processes."

"What about that green folder?" asked Barry, pointing. "Is that a list of things we are doing right?"

"Have you ever known an auditor give you a pat on the back? This miscolored folder is actually a list of problems in our documentation that we just talked about. The folder is chock full of examples, such as multiple and inconsistent price lists, missing supplier contracts, outdated marketing plan codes, missing policy documents, and so on."

Barry reached out for a folder in red. He thumbed through it, mumbling out rapidly for Dan's benefit. "This one goes into excruciating detail about our inability to locate key documents in a timely manner. This is a thrilling story about our lack of a document management process."

"Here's a detailed description of problems in our operational processes," said Dan, pulling out a violet folder. "These are all concerned with too many people touching the same data too many times. There is no controllership over how the data gets modified at all the various parts of the process."

Barry nodded thoughtfully. "I know what you mean. Our salespeople promise the customer certain terms; these terms get shot down by our underwriters. The documentation coordinators modify those terms further, depending on whether the customer provides additional information or not. The shipping clerk may or may not package all the manuals if he or she doesn't get them on time. The shipping department is heavily penalized for missing a ship date, so they ship the material out even if it is incomplete."

"You know the salespeople promise just about anything to get the deal," said Dan, irritably. "Sometimes the economics of the deal are terrible, so somebody has to throw cold water on the idea."

"I know," said Barry, with a slight smile. "I used to be in sales myself, remember?" He pawed around the piles. "Looks like we are done with these colorful folders. What do you think we should do?"

"Do we have any choice? Start with folder number one, page one, item one, examine it in detail, identify an owner to address the issue. Then we move on to item number two on page one of folder number one. And so on."

"And you think that'll address the problem?"

"Sure. Not my idea of work-life-spirit balance, of course."

"And you are sure these issue won't come back to haunt us next year?"

"At this point I am not sure of my own name. No, I can't guarantee non-recurrence."

Barry got up and walked over to the window, staring out across the harbor. A brisk wind billowed out the many white sails taking full advantage of the weather. Barry wished he was out there, sails fluttering, wind in his hair, a salty tang on his lips, his ears resonating with the musical, sibilant whoosh of the waves washing by, the air resounding with the strident squawking of the sea-gulls, his legs bending and straightening like stabilizers keeping his upper body relatively motionless. He missed the feeling of effortless oneness, a sense of psychosensual flow, what the Japanese called *shibumi*. He turned back towards Dan.

"I don't think we should rush into this," he said. "We do it to ourselves all the time. We madly dash about putting out a fire, then another one starts out somewhere else. I once patched the bottom of my sail boat when I was a callow, inexperienced youth. I disdained professional help, and tried to do it all by myself. When I was done, I brashly took it out into the water. You ever get stuck in the middle of the bay with tiny fountains springing up faster than you could plug them?"

"We have only one month to come up with a plan," warned Dan. "This is no time to reminisce about badly fixed sail boats."

"No, but it is the right time to reflect on the lessons learned from that incident. We should address the root causes of all these problems." Barry tapped the stack of folders. "The next time I do not want to see such folders on my desk."

"Do I detect a five year plan coming up?"

"I hope not. The way I figure it, our processes are broken. Even our processes about our processes are broken. We should address those. Not run around fixing one tactical item after another endlessly."

"But the devil is in the details. Ultimately we have to look at these items line by line and respond to them."

"Oh yes, we will. But we will do it in the context of a well-thought out plan, not a knee-jerk reaction to the legislation of the day."

"Alright. You have a plan. Care to share it with me?"

"This whole story smells of broken processes."

"Do I detect the panacea of BPM creeping in?"

"Don't be so skeptical, Dan. Think about it! BPM is the one methodology—or whatever the heck it is—where the emphasis is all about who does what to whom, how they do it, how to best document it, how to establish controls to detect it, and how to manage it to make sure that everything doesn't go to the Hades in a handbasket."

"Alright, as long as we don't fool ourselves that if we only buy a BPM solution all our problems are solved. Be forewarned that I'm going to rein Jeff in pretty sharply if he gets on his hobby horse and claims that BPM will fix all this," said Dan, sharply tapping one of the audit files.

"Agreed." Barry took a deep breath. "Let's see what our friendly neighborhood consultant has to say about this."

Barry stepped up to his desk and picked up the phone.

* * *

Barry was seated regally behind his imposing desk. Arranged around him were Dan, Marty, Carl, Mark, and Chuck. Barry had deliberately devised a somber and subdued effect, as befitted a mournful examination of the ruinous results of an internal audit. He also wanted to forestall any razzle-dazzle from Jeff.

Jeff took in all this almost immediately the moment he walked in. He broke up Barry's meticulously engineered effect by walking diagonally over to the large window overlooking the harbor.

"Oh boy! Look at that view!" he said, in a loud, bubbling voice that clashed violently with the funereal atmosphere. "Look at those sail boats! What's that strange looking boat?" he asked, pointing.

Barry couldn't resist it anymore. He popped out of his chair and joined Jeff at the window.

"Oh, that one! It is a replica of one of the most famous Chinese junks, called the Keying..." he began excitedly. He stopped, as the threnody of four throats in the throes of a fit of coughing assaulted him. "Eh, sorry...need to get back to business."

He cupped a hand under Jeff's elbow and steered him back to the conference table.

"I know you have some ideas. You sounded pretty sure on the phone," he asked Jeff, when they were all seated.

"I have an idea that your idea has to do with BPM," piped up Dan.

"I have bad news for you," said Jeff, coolly settling down into his chair. "BPM will not solve all these problems."

Dan felt deflated. He had carefully built up and rehearsed his scathing speech to bring Jeff down to earth from a BPM utopia in the sky. He glanced wistfully at his notes. He tried to salvage an argument. "You are not saying that a full implementation of BPM will address these issues?"

"Nein," said Jeff shortly.

"You are not claiming that BPM will force correct alignment of people to functions?"

"Nyet."

"You are not suggesting that BPM will ensure that people work efficiently with no wasted activities?"

"Non."

"You are not advising me that BPM will enforce complete monitoring of all wayward transactions?"

"Iye."

"Speak English, will you!"

Jeff leaned forward. "I meant, no, N-O," he said, emphasizing each letter by banging his fist on the table. "I just wanted to see if giving you a negative answer in any other language made it more palatable."

"It doesn't, unfortunately. So, BPM can't help us. Pity, I was looking for any help I could get," said Dan mournfully.

"Ah, that's where you err, O Master Cruncher of Numbers! BPM can definitely help."

"What's with all that no-no-ing then?"

Jeff looked around the room at them. "I see that you may have zigged while I zagged, semantically speaking. You are looking for a tool that will single-handedly solve your problems. I'm proposing that no such magical tool exists, much as the vendors would like to claim otherwise. BPM helps you make tremendous progress; it provides a framework for a solution; it gives you a process to keep your business processes in control—what I call a *meta-process*. But to make it all succeed, people have to apply the methodology, use the tools, be diligent about documenting what they do, and have the discipline to update the process documentation when things do change."

Dan gently drummed his fingers on the cover of his HP calculator. "I can understand that," he said. "People cannot leave their brains behind, assuming that BPM will take care of everything."

"Precisely. Remember, I do claim that BPM will kick the intellectual content of people's activities up a notch. It will improve productivity, remove drudgery, and build capacity into your organization."

"Okay, we get the big vision," said Barry. "Actually we are glad you are a realist about this BPM. I have to admit we were afraid we would be dealing with a fanatic."

"I quite understand," replied Jeff. "I can't say this enough: BPM is not a glib answer to all the ills of homo sapiens. The most important idea of BPM is the process mindset. I know the term 'process' is overused, but it essentially means a way of doing something. It is a formula or a recipe. The more specific meaning of the term is the total context under which tasks are carried out in sequence or in parallel, synchronously or asynchronously, to achieve a business objective. I won't pretend to advise you on how to run your business or make money. You wouldn't be where you are if you didn't know how. But I suggest that the most important objective you have is customer satisfaction."

"Our customers will go into raptures to hear you say that," said Barry. "You'll get no argument from us on that score. What does that have to do with our internal processes? Tell us how you might approach this problem with our internal controls."

Jeff patted the stack of audit report folders. "Can you give me one example of one line item in these folders that, if you didn't fix, will not impact your customers? I'd suggest that you prioritize this list by ignoring all such non-customer centric audit issues from phase I of your process engineering."

The group leaned back, trying to come up with examples that would not touch the customer. Marty picked up a folder at random and started thumbing through it. Others followed his example. Only Barry pursed his lips and looked at Jeff with a mildly quizzical expression.

"Now that you put it like that," said Carl slowly, "I can't see one item here that does not somehow impact customers. Of course," he continued quickly, "some have a direct influence on the customers, and some indirectly affect the customer."

"Let me ask you a different question," pursued Jeff. "Assume Sarbanes-Oxley regulation did not exist, FASB—the Financial Accounting Standards Board—guidelines did not exist, Anti-Money Laundering or Know Your Customer did not exist. Would you still establish these controls?"

"Never," retorted Marty.

"I'm not sure," said Dan. "I know these regulations are a big nuisance, but at the end of the day, they do force excellent internal controllership. It's only when they are enforced on us by an external Big Brother that we rebel against them."

"Excellent! That's what I was hoping to hear. Forget the issue of regulation for a minute. Think of the controllership you want on your ship. Think of how tautly Barry controls his boat. That's how he wins those races. You always need to control your ship. What's debatable is what methods you employ. You can choose to breathe down your employees' necks every minute, hold endless meetings, fill out forms and reports to death, or you can choose the saner alternative: take a close look at your processes—continually—and learn to incorporate and manage controls in a disciplined way."

"Great suggestion," chimed in Barry. "Now, cut to the chase. Give us some specific ideas. What is this going to cost? How long will it take?"

"What is that 'it' that you are looking for?"

"Why, the system to automate these controls, of course."

"Would you buy just any old sail for your boat?"

"Oh no, I'd look at it pretty closely to make sure it isn't full of holes and won't come apart at the seams."

"Isn't it also just as important to know your own boat well before outfitting it with sails? Shouldn't the sails be just the right size and number for the dimensions of your boat?"

"Definitely. Let me see if I can translate that. You are asking us to understand our processes better before running to the corner drugstore and buying any old software."

"That is correct. There is simply no shortcut around it."

"Everything seems to come back to the need for documenting our processes."

"That is the correct first step. Whether you like it not, you will be forced to come back to the basic question: do I really understand my business processes."

Carl had enough of the call to basics. "But why couldn't we just bring in that compliance solutions vendor who gave us a call the other day? They claimed that their software has all the compliance metrics built into it. All we need to do is start using it."

Marty perked up. "That would be the worst thing to do. Think ERP implementations! Remember how much work we had to do after we signed the contract for that general ledger system? It had nothing to do with installing the software and converting data. We spent months trying to figure out exactly how our processes work, what the data definitions meant, how information flows, who does what, and a thousand other issues like that."

Carl was thoughtful. "I see the point. There is really no shortcut around acquiring a thorough understanding of processes."

"The thing I don't understand," chimed in Chuck, "is that our processes change all the time, some of them more rapidly than others. The moment we document a process it becomes obsolete."

"That is like claiming you don't have time to exercise," responded Jeff. "You *always* have the time; the question is, are you going to allot the time to your hobby or whatever you think you should be doing, or will you let something else control your time? Let me give you all a couple of thoughts on this issue of continuous and rapid change of processes."

Jeff walked over to the whiteboard set in one of the side walls.

He wrote a large 'A' on it, and drew a circle around the letter.

"Firstly, I'll guarantee that documenting a new process or updating the documentation on an existing one is always going to be faster than the change in the underlying business process itself. Your business processes really don't change once every week, do they?"

There were negative shakes of the head around the table.

Jeff wrote 'Processes change' below the 'A.' Then he inscribed a large 'B' beside the 'A,' and drew a circle around it too.

"Secondly, you spend a significant portion of each project trying to nail down the existing process; without that understanding, you don't know what to change or how to change it. This is the single biggest mistake people—especially the IT folks—make, namely, promising new implementations without budgeting adequate time to gain an understanding of the current reality."

"Wait a minute!" protested Marty. "The deadlines are pushed onto IT by the business."

"True enough," said Jeff, writing 'Current processes' below the 'B.' "But I think IT could do a lot more to push back. We'll cover this later. The point I'm trying to make is that buying that latest cool application will rarely solve the problem."

"Just the point I was trying to make," muttered Marty.

"Never mind, scratch the vendor and their application for now," said Barry. "I agree that we senior managers hear about these vendor offerings all the time, especially at the 19th hole. I must admit the blandishments are quite powerful."

"I am not saying you shouldn't buy some of these applications. After all, the vendors do put a lot of thought into them. For emerging fields, the vendors are almost certainly going to be thought leaders. Just as the auto companies pioneer new designs and new engines, these vendors push the limits of new ideas into software."

"Wait, I am confused," said Dan. "I thought you were down on the vendors. Now you are calling them thought leaders."

Carl, who was into cars, jumped in. "I think I'm beginning to understand Jeff's point. The auto magazines praise a new model to the sky, and it's pretty heady stuff. However, I don't rush out to buy the latest model. Firstly, I couldn't afford it. Secondly, even if I am in the market for a new car, I would have to first understand my own needs, and perform a match between the features of the new models and my needs before I plunk down serious cash."

"Okay, we've established that we don't just want to rush out and get the latest compliance software. What now?" asked Barry.

"First, start a serious effort to use BPM tools to document your processes," advised Jeff. He put a check mark below the circled 'B' on the whiteboard. "That should challenge the issue that you have no time to do this. You'll find out soon enough that not only do you have enough time, but you also start acquiring a stronger understanding of your processes."

"But," protested Chuck. "There are thousands of processes! We can't stop all work and start drawing process maps."

"You can't possibly have thousands of processes. Your business can't be all that complicated! Never mind. I know you meant that figuratively. But you do have a good point. I would definitely not advocate that you stop your routine business for this effort. To make headway here, you have two pragmatic options. One, you could look for critical processes and start with those. Two, you could institute a disciplined approach to process mapping for the currently active projects. I am sure that at this moment you have a few projects just starting off, or those that just got started. Apply the principles of business process modeling with those. That should address the issue of processes changing before you can capture them." Jeff put a check mark against the 'A.'

"I like that approach," said Barry. "But how does that exactly address compliance? What do we do with these stacks of adverse audit reports?"

"If you inaugurate a new mindset that you care about diligence in documenting processes, that would be a good start. The ostensible stick you should use is non-compliance. But to truly address compliance issues, you should train your analysts to ask intelligent questions about control points. Assign one employee from every function to work on compliance. Next, train all the compliance people plus all your business analysts and process analysts on the

COSO framework."

"And that is?"

"COSO stands for 'The Committee of Sponsoring Organizations,' a product of the Treadway Commission. The framework addresses financial reporting, compliance, operational efficiency, and operational effectiveness. A very important point made by the COSO framework is that internal control is a process itself. It is not something you institute once and be done with it. I am sure all of you realize that conceptually. But the way to make it an everyday reality is to apply the ideas of BPM to it."

"You quoted from Warren Buffet about costs in one of our first meetings, Jeff. I liked it a lot. What was it again?" asked Barry.

"The good manager does not wake up one day and say to himself, 'I'm going to manage costs today.' Costs should be managed every moment."

"I love it!" said Barry, thumping the table. "I guess we could say the same thing of internal controls."

"Managing regulation is going to become a full-time affair for everyone in the company!" complained Carl.

"Don't look at it negatively," said Barry. "Let's ignore regulation for a minute. The COSO framework looks useful from an internal perspective."

Jeff put in, "To paraphrase Warren Buffet, 'The good manager does not wake up one day and say to himself, 'I'm going to manage risk today.' Enterprise risk should be managed everyday. Instead of going after growth at any price, you should go after responsible growth."

"We don't want another Enron or MCI/Worldcom type of situation," said Marty.

"Oh, come now!" burst out Dan. "Our company is hardly engaged in any shenanigans."

"I am sure your company is not doing anything unethical," said Jeff. "But the way things are going in Wall Street, negligence or incompetence is going to be viewed as if it were fraud. It really pays to be extra diligent, and the way to do that efficiently and systematically is to use business process management."

"So, I think we got the first order of business figured out," said Barry, briskly rubbing his hands. "Chuck, could you take the lead and draft out a communication about establishing a process mindset? We'll all review it at our next weekly staff meeting and wordsmith it if necessary. Then, I'll send it out to the whole company."

"Don't forget to mention the compliance angle," advised Dan.

"We may need a good catch phrase," mused Mark Andersen, the VP of Marketing. "Something like, *Keep Your CEO and CFO out of jail.*"

Barry laughed. "Save your marketing one-liners for the business, Mark. Let's keep this communication constructive. It should be viewed as a proactive measure."

"It should actually herald a change in company culture," said Jeff. "Moving to a process mindset is very difficult and non-intuitive for many people, since they are so used to working in functional organizations."

"Uh oh, he wants to get rid of us functional managers next," quipped Carl.

"All in good time," retorted Jeff, with a wink. "I am going to strongly recommend that you move to a value-process organization."

"In the meantime...," ventured Marty.

"On to the next thing you should do to satisfy your auditors and your Board one hundred percent," said Jeff. "Change your project management processes to show that process controllership is now part and parcel of how projects are conducted. Your Board and the auditors should realize you are serious about this. As projects go through each tollgate, they should comply with a checklist of process-related questions. So, the second thing you should do is create the right checklists that will ensure controllership in your project execution."

Barry turned to Marty. "I'd like you to take the lead on this one. Project management falls squarely into IT's competency. As a function, you folks do more project work than anyone else."

"Got it, Barry. I'll have a draft for you for our next staff meeting."

"Shouldn't we discuss how to address the compliance violations?" asked Dan.

Jeff answered, "The first two steps of your plan should be communicating the vision of a process mindset, and formalizing the controllership part of your delivery or execution mechanism. I suggest that your next (third) step is to identify critical processes where compliance is an issue. Don't worry so much which process has the most number of violations. Focus instead on those processes that are directly related to financial reporting or those that touch your customers directly, and which also have the more serious violations. Those should be addressed first."

Barry turned to Dan. "Do you think you can have a prioritized list of such processes to review at our staff meeting?"

"Yes, that should not be a problem. I spent the whole weekend poring over these reports. I have a decent handle on what I think we should tackle first."

"Aren't we forgetting the actual BPM tools that will help us?"

"Why can't we use our traditional drawing tool, Microsoft PowerPoint?" asked Chuck. "We are all pretty comfortable with that."

Marty shuddered. "Aw, come on, Chuck. PowerPoint is a great tool for presentations, but do you really want our analysts to spend their time drawing boxes, lines, decision diamonds, and so on? What about the time it takes to pretty up the process maps? I really think we should use Visio."

Jeff simulated an exaggerated shudder. "Visio is a great tool for ad-hoc drawings, but I really suggest that you invest in a good process mapping tool. You will get so much more productivity out of a true process modeling tool that it'll pay for itself on your very first project. By the way, if Microsoft ever figured out how to make Visio a true BPM tool, they could walk away with a multi-billion dollar pot of platinum."

"Jeff, do we wait for Microsoft to get their act together, or can you suggest a few of these BPM tools? I'd like to see pros and cons for each of these tools, and a comparison with Visio and Power-Point. Let's review that as a group at our staff meeting next week."

"You got it, Barry," said Jeff.

"Looks like next week's staff meeting is going to be focused on BPM and Compliance. You want to send out an email to the rest of the staff highlighting that theme?" suggested Dan.

"Excellent idea. I'll summarize what we discussed here today. I'll ask everyone to come forward with thoughts. I really want us to finalize our plan of attack at that staff meeting."

Dan looked visibly excited. "If we come to an agreement at the staff meeting, we should fill in the details within the next couple of weeks. We should be ready to submit a credible plan to the Board and our internal audit team by end of the month."

"That should beat the one month deadline by a week," said Barry. "Like Superman, BPM comes to the rescue once again."

Jeff laughed. "Not just yet. In the next few weeks, Superman will be busy changing into his BPM suit. The actual rescue is yet to take place. This is such a difficult problem that even Superman needs a few months to solve it."

"Come on, Jeff, do your aphorism thing again," said Marty.

Jeff looked at them sitting around the table. They were all smiling, waiting expectantly. He thought for a moment.

"I venture Sterllings' Theorem on Compliance: *Business Process Management offers a disciplined, sustainable metaprocess for controllership and compliance.*"

"And your inevitable corollary?" prodded Marty.

"Ah yes, the corollary. One of these days I'll run out corollaries, and then I'll get a coronary. But here's one for now," said Jeff. He recited:

If whips and chains ain't your thing,
Come give BPM a fling.

Key Points

- Controllership and compliance should not be approached with a knee-jerk reaction to external regulation, but in the context of a disciplined approach.
- Understanding internal business processes thoroughly is a necessary condition for attaining true controllership.
- BPM, as a technology, cannot by itself solve problems of controllership; the right culture and discipline are necessary.
- BPM provides a framework and the tools to gain and maintain process knowledge.
- Study and follow the COSO (Committee of Sponsoring Organizations) framework for managing enterprise risk.
- Formulate and communicate a process mindset.
- Incorporate controllership into the execution and review mechanisms of the business.

14 United We Stand

Jeff helped himself to one more jelly donut and took a sip of the coffee. He turned towards the speaker at his elbow.

"I'm sorry, I didn't quite catch that," he said.

"I was asking you what you thought about the open source movement. Should we be looking at some of the open source BPM software, such as…"

"We can discuss open source, but I'm more interested in advocating an open mind about change," said Jeff, gently interrupting what promised to be a technology hobby horse.

He found himself surrounded by a small group of men and women, all carrying coffee, donuts, and bagels. A little farther away, a line was slowly moving along a table set with a continental breakfast. The random social chit-chat was quieting down, and Jeff found himself at the locus of their gathering attention.

"The challenge most companies face is not so much in the actual technology itself," Jeff continued, "but in the processes that surround it. A good analogy is how radiology departments are structured in modern hospitals. The actual investigative procedures take very little time, but the workflow processes that move patients in and out are still inefficient."

"It's debatable whether you would want them to get more efficient," observed Chuck, who had joined the group. "Doctors have already lost their bedside manner, because the HMOs now manage everything by numbers. Humans need a bit more handholding and mollycoddling."

"You are so right," said Jeff. He gestured to the large conference table and parked himself into the nearest chair. The employees from PIQ and IT quickly settled down around him.

"I guess we just called the meeting to order," observed Marty. "Let's go around the room and introduce ourselves. Everyone, tell your name, your function, and what you expect to get out of this meeting."

The introductions were quickly performed. Jeff made short notes while they spoke. When they were done, he glanced at his notes, and addressed them.

"It looks like the room is more or less evenly divided between PIQ and IT people. I heard the following expectations from you: the PIQ folks want to understand what the big fuss is about process management and all the new technology; you IT guys want to understand why the PIQ guys are so darn snooty."

There was uneasy laughter and wry smiles around the room. Jeff detected an undercurrent of polarization. Jeff glanced meaningfully at Marty and Chuck.

"Oh yes," said Marty. "Chuck and I will leave you now. We want you all to be unrestrained and open. We will mop up the blood, er...I mean, debrief, after the meeting. Have fun!"

Nodding at Jeff, he sauntered out of the room.

"Yes, ask this man anything you like," said Chuck. "But just be careful, don't sign up to go on any lean diets!"

Waving cheerily at the group, Chuck leisurely waddled out of the room.

Jeff turned to the two teams.

"Being open reminds me of the main topic I wanted to bring up," he began. "One of you asked me about my opinion of open source. Interesting as that subject is, the trickier problem is to motivate change. Just now, I gave you a tongue-in-cheek recap of your expectations. Did I miss anything? Anyone want to add anything?"

They all looked at each other, but no one volunteered to add or modify anything.

Jeff continued, "In that case, let us take the first issue. IT feels that the black belts play rough with them. What type of behavior from the PIQ group would facilitate a better relationship with IT?"

One of the business analysts spoke up. "I'd like to know about process improvement projects that black belts work on."

Another added, "I'd like to be part of the project team right from the beginning, not just when the improvements have to be digitized."

Jeff asked the PIQ team, "Would you have any concerns about

not inviting the IT folks to your project meetings?"

A black belt sitting at the far end answered. "In principle, we don't want to exclude anyone. But everyone must understand that the Six Sigma methodology is very specific. There is a process to follow, tools to use, and artifacts to produce. I'm not sure if the time of the IT team is wisely spent at out PIQ meetings. After all, we don't insist on being part of IT's design sessions."

Another black belt chimed in, nodding her head. "IT design is not our area of competence, and I, for one, am not ashamed to admit it."

A seasoned IT project manager burst out, "But if we don't get involved up front, we can't manage the quality of requirements."

A master black belt frowned at the IT project manager. "What do you mean? That we don't produce high quality requirements? That's unlikely, given the fact that we *are* the Quality group."

"Perhaps I should have said, *the requirements are not detailed and complete enough.* As a high-level description of an improved process, they are fine. But we can't build our systems based on high-level descriptions. We need to get down to the bare metal."

"But that," pointed out another master black belt, "defeats the purpose of our PIQ project meetings. The goal is not to dive into the data-field level of detail."

Jeff interjected. "I love the energy you are all displaying about this issue. If you don't mind, let me summarize the issue. Then I'll propose a solution, okay?"

There were relieved nods around the table.

"Regardless of what IT or Quality wants," continued Jeff, "the main goal of each group is to have access to the information they need to perform their jobs. Right?"

Murmurs of 'right,' 'you got it,' 'exactly,' etc. floated around the table.

"Since you are all part of one company, you also have another goal that is very close to the first one: to ensure that the work you do can be leveraged by the other party. I would assume you don't want to just perform your own job with no regard for the consequences to others."

This time the agreement was more vociferous.

"Excellent!" said Jeff. "I can see that your hearts are in the right place. The one caveat you have not stated but I am sure is uppermost in your mind right now is this: you are willing to change the way you operate if it will benefit the other team only if it does not detract you from your first goal."

One of the master black belts spoke up. "I'm relieved to hear you say that. Every time I think of that caveat, I don't articulate it. I worry that I will come across as a bad corporate citizen."

An IT project manager agreed. "From our side, we don't want to come across as making PIQ do our job for us, or to look like we'd accept freebies from them. We do want to take on more responsibility. We are proud of our roles."

Jeff laughed. "You should take a job in public relations. Your remarks should be chiseled on a marble plaque."

The atmosphere in the room lightened. Suddenly, everyone felt they were jelling into one team. Jeff took advantage of the change in the mood. He walked over to a flip chart set up in one corner.

"I propose the following Three Laws of Organizational Synergy," he said, writing on the flip chart. A couple of employees helped tape the pages up on the wall. When he was done, they all digested in meditative silence the three laws that Jeff proposed:

The First Law
Employees shall be diligent and focused in the performance of their primary job tasks.

The Second Law
Employees shall innovate and improve processes, except when this conflicts with the First Law.

The Third Law
Employees shall perform their tasks in a way that provides efficiencies to their colleagues, unless such performance conflicts with the First or Second Law.

"Interesting," said a master black belt. "There is a certain symmetry to the laws."

"Each builds on the preceding one," added a business analyst.

"Except, of course, the first," amended another business analyst, pedantically.

"And they establish the priorities," observed a project manager.

"That is the general idea," said Jeff. "Management books, consultants, and theories all talk about cooperation and synergy. They don't address the reality that companies drive priorities from the top down, while the focus on execution happens from the ground up."

"They look cutely organized," observed a technical architect. "But I'm not sure I fully understand."

"Let me clarify," replied Jeff. "The First Law is the real tactical motivation for all companies, regardless of how much the top management chatters about innovation, competitive advantage, and other mantras. Without performing the minimum necessary to sustain the fundamental business model, no amount of high-falutin' talk will save the company from ruin.

"The Second Law puts innovation and process improvement into perspective. Innovation is innovation of, and from, the basic business model. If your basic business is non-existent, there will not be anything to innovate. The second law exhorts you to not keep your heads in the clouds.

"The Third Law describes the context of collaboration and team work. It cautions you not to go about helping others at the expense of your own responsibilities. It preaches enlightened self-interest, not self-destructive altruism."

"Isn't the Third Law justifying a siloed attitude? We have so much work to do that we can always justify not helping others. One could always cop out."

"That would be irrational behavior. The law assumes that employees are rational individuals who understand that business processes are not one-directional."

"You mean, what goes around comes around?" asked a testing expert.

"How can that be?" protested a data architect. "Business processes start at origination or when parts arrive from suppliers, and end with fulfillment or shipping."

Jeff knew he had to clarify this point. It was critical to the spirit of BPM. "What happens if fulfillment is not carried out in a timely way?" he asked.

"The customer gets hopping mad."

"Is the customer likely to repeat his or her business with you?"

"Only if they forget the bad episode."

"More importantly, is the customer likely to promote your company with his or her contacts?"

"Not likely."

"So what does that do to repeat business?"

The teams nodded at each other in understanding.

"Let me emphasize this principle: business processes should have feedback mechanisms. This is well known in manufacturing businesses, because people can see parts moving through manufacturing lines. However, it is not well-recognized in service businesses, because the items of interest are not physical parts but paper, electronic documents, and nebulous metrics."

A master black belt, who had been silent until now, cleared her throat. The room fell silent, and everyone turned to her attentively. Evidently she was deeply respected by her colleagues.

"It seems to me," she began, her voice soft yet arresting, "that the Third Law ensures that we don't optimize processes solely at the functional level. Not only does the Third Law advocate cooperation, but it also exhorts us to synchronize our oars in the water."

Jeff smiled. "That's an interesting way to put it. You are absolutely right, of course. Mathematicians have a fancy way of stating what you just said. They speak of optimizing processes either locally or globally. It is well-known, at least to mathematicians, that a series of locally optimal solutions do not necessarily create a globally optimal solution. In fact, they could very well lead to a series of unfortunate events. The Third Law is therefore saying, go ahead and optimize your processes, but first make sure you are not creating inefficiencies somewhere else."

"Can you give us some practical advice on how we can all work together more effectively, Jeff?"

"That's the major strength of process management. BPM offers you not just the theory and fancy talk, but also provides very specific tools and techniques to ensure there is true coordination and synergy."

Some of the black belts looked at each other in confusion. What was this? An IT tool that facilitates coordination and synergy? Jeff observed their blank looks.

"I'll explain how it really works," he said soothingly. "First, though, is each of you willing to make a few changes so that you can follow the spirit of the three laws?"

"I don't know if I really want to learn to write code," grumbled one of the black belts.

"I quit B-school because I didn't really like statistics," confessed an IT designer.

"Nothing as drastic as that," said Jeff. "There would be small changes in the way you work, small skills and tools that you'd pick up."

The seasoned master black belt that they all respected said, her face wreathed in smiles. "I think you'd better explain the nitty-gritty, Jeff. Even snooty statisticians can be insecure."

"Very well. The question that is uppermost in most people's minds when they hear about something new like this is, *cui bono*? Or, who benefits from this? As we continue our discussion, keep your focus on that question and compile a list of benefits that would apply to you in your role.

"For starters, I ask that the PIQ folks learn to use sophisticated process modeling and analysis tools in your daily work. I know you are all familiar with statistical simulation tools, but you should also use process-based simulation tools. By using formal tools for process modeling, you will be forced—I employ the word *force* in a positive sense—to use standardized notation and symbols that will be recognized by your IT counterparts. The standardized notation is called BPMN, or Business Process Modeling Notation. You will also become very disciplined in thinking about control points, spec limits for processes, and so on. After all, you go through a lot of pain in your statistical analysis and in creating the improved processes. Why not ensure that the processes stay in control by communicating those control limits to IT so that IT can digitize and automatically track them?"

"You mean we could build dashboards based on the control points?" asked one of the IT project managers.

"Yes, that is correct. The requirement for the PIQ organization to learn new skills ends there. No need to learn anything about technology, you see!"

"Are these process modeling tools part of the BPM platform?" asked one of the black belts, apprehensively.

"You look like you are being led to the slaughter house! Do you know how to use a simple application like Visio? Good! Then you could easily learn to use the process modeling tool that comes with a leading BPM platform."

"Is that going to be the extent of our exposure to BPM?" asked a black belt suspiciously. "There is no phase two where we are supposed to pick up one more teeny skill like, say, Java programming?"

"Nope. Word of honor."

"How exactly does this promote cooperation between PIQ and IT?"

"I think I see it," said one business analyst. He turned to face his PIQ colleagues. "The usual way we operate is that you guys create your process maps on paper, transcribe it to MS Word or Visio documents. Then you shoot them across to us. We try to make some sense out of them. We don't understand how the business transactions flow across the processes, or how the data gets transformed. Your process maps are mostly at too high a level for our use. We have to go back and interview the same business users that you interviewed. I don't know if you realize this, but the business users always say to us, 'How come you are asking us all these questions? We just explained it all to the PIQ guys. Why don't you go ask them?' By using standard process modeling tools, you could easily capture some of that information the first time."

"That is a very good way to state it," agreed Jeff. "I want you all to think about the different informational layers in business processes. Each layer deals with one perspective, and has one category of information that is relevant. The PIQ team is primarily interested in statistical data and statistical analysis. Along the way, they capture data about roles, high-level business transactions, locations, business rules, and so on."

Another black belt had an epiphany. "I suppose the same process model where we capture all that information would be used by the business analysts to capture and analyze the next layer of information about that process. Am I right?"

"Absolutely correct!" exclaimed Jeff, pleased with their insights. "You are on the right track. The business analysts would now delve into the details of data fields, the business rules that speak to the actual data coming from or stored in systems, the manual artifacts that the business users employ, and other myriad details. The PIQ team would inform the business users that the work of the PIQ department covers only one aspect of business processes. They'd set expectations with their clients that the business analysts and the IT organization would follow up with them for details that are necessary for implementing the improved process."

"All this is well and good for the PIQ and business analyst teams," said one of the technical architects. "Could you explain if there is any gravy in all this for us techies?"

"Definitely! Let's review how you might use all this information and continue to dive into the information layers. Technical architects are concerned about design. They want to marry up the requirements to specific technical artifacts, such as use cases, object models, component models, database schemas, web services, and so on. Now imagine that each of the process steps outlined by the black belt and described in detail by the business analyst must be digitized. A technical designer has all the information he or she needs to use in their design."

One of the other technical architects tapped her notepad thoughtfully. "I see how the upfront process work could be used. We have a ready-made specification of the business data, the flow of information between various systems or between manual artifacts as the case may be, as well as the detailed business rules. We also know who the actors are..." she broke off, turned towards the PIQ team and said, "Sorry, the word *actor* refers to the primary subject of a use case. Usually, the actor is a role, but sometimes it could be a system."

"I guess we could use the detailed sub-processes to describe the detailed scenarios and exceptions," put in one of the developers.

"You are getting it," said Jeff, happy with the change in the atmosphere. They were all trying to find ways to work on a common platform. "The other benefit is that the business analyst would have described the business transactions that can be used for object modeling and data modeling. The process steps yield a clue towards the actual methods that can be implemented in the object model. There is a strong correlation between the process model and the design level models."

"If that is the case, are tools available to facilitate the conversion of process models into design?"

"You are in luck. The field has matured considerably by moving to one standard, called BPEL, or Business Process Execution Language. Just as BPMN is a standard way to use symbols for documenting process flows, BPEL is a standard way to specify design level models. Good BPM platforms automatically produce BPEL specifications from the process models. The BPEL model, which is actually an XML document, is coupled with a WSDL document, or Web Services Description Language. These two documents, the BPEL and the WSDL, provide a detailed specification of the design models and the services that could be used to implement the processes. By the way, WSDL itself is an XML-based specification. The only caution I have for you techies is that both BPMN and BPEL are still evolving, so make sure you keep a close watch on them."

The technical team looked visibly excited. Here was the real stuff! They understood the importance of change, communication, coordination, and other soft organizational issues, but the systems-level talk got their juices really flowing.

"Is this what is meant by Service-Oriented Architecture?"

"It is only one aspect of it," cautioned Jeff. "I consider SOA to be a most important—in fact, invaluable—adjunct to good business process design. After all, why would you build a technical service that does not explicitly map to a business process? Conversely, why go through the pain of all that process documentation and analysis if you couldn't somehow take advantage of your IT systems?"

One of the master black belts made an unexpected and surprising observation. "It almost seems that first we must define business services, and use that definition to build technical services."

"Very perceptive," said Jeff. "In some cases, a process step may clearly map into a business service. At other times, two or more process steps may be defined as one business service. Finally, a high-level process step may be described by more than one business service. A similar many-to-many relationship may exist between business services and technical services."

A project manager, with an aptitude for synthesizing a complete picture out of multiple, related concepts, offered his view. "It is clear that this methodology allows analysis at multiple levels: the process level, the business services level, and the technical services level. Moreover, all these levels and all the information are tied to one single underlying model."

Jeff corroborated, adding, "A good BPM platform will yield up a bonus benefit: each type of user will be able to view the process and its information from their own perspective. Such a BPM platform will ensure that each user is not deluged with excessive and unnecessary information."

The project manager followed up with a question that was troubling him. "I like the way process management and SOA bring together the multiple models and layers of abstraction. I feel a little uneasy about one issue, though. How seamlessly can one move from one to the other in the technical domain? I mean, don't we have to use the syntax of the implementation technology? When we need to migrate to a different technology platform, or mix and match various systems and applications, don't we have to redesign the architecture, or at least maintain different version of it?"

Jeff responded thoughtfully, "You hit upon one of the most critical problems in technical architecture. Those of you in Quality may not appreciate it so much because you don't encounter it first-hand, but the issue is that architectural specifications end up being written using the constructs of the implementation technology. This is a bit like using the US system of measurement for your house plans. Usually works fine, but what if you bought the design from an architect in UK? What if you then wanted to add a Japanese garden using a design from a Japanese architect? What with translating from the metric system and the Japanese language, your contractor might quit on you! As if this headache were not enough, it can get worse. If the plumbers and the carpenters, for example, do not share a common vocabulary or meta-model, the carpenters may not make allowances for some of the properties of plumbing components, such as heat generation and overflow."

An architect spoke up. "It is almost like translating between two languages. Even though dictionaries for both languages exist, the multiple semantics, homonyms, idioms, and so on, can make this a tricky problem."[59]

"Excellent analogy," said Jeff. "If two different systems or implementation technologies shared a metamodel with precise mappings to each other, and if the specifications for both the systems were complete, exhaustive, and used the metamodel constructs, then it would be easy to move from one to the other.[60] A good solution in IT is to introduce an abstraction layer that allows you to

---

[59] For some hilarious examples, see Tom Dillon's *Japanese Made Funny (Gaijin Bloops in Nihongo)*.

[60] For a detailed treatment of MDA, see *Real-Life MDA: Solving Business Problems with Model-Driven Architecture*, by Michael Guttman & John Parodi.

model the architecture in a way that is independent of the implementation technology."

"I assume this marvel of an abstraction layer has an acronym?" quipped a Six Sigma expert.

Jeff laughed. "It's de rigueur! This breakthrough idea is called MDA, or Model-Driven Architecture. It provides a standards-based framework for the interoperability of many IT models. It allows for what is known as 'separation of concerns,' meaning that varying levels of abstraction concern themselves with various aspects of IT architecture."[61]

One veteran programmer spoke up. "I hear a lot about agility. I am thinking this is a lot of hot air, and just boils down to longer working hours. What are your thoughts, Jeff?"

"It is not hype at all, though an unclear understanding of agility on the part of the management can leave you with that impression. The prerequisites for a truly agile organization are, firstly, a process culture; secondly, good discipline and skills in process modeling and information architecture; thirdly, a solid understanding of the new—and some not so new—concepts of technology, such as SOA, design models, use cases, UML, BPEL, XML, extreme programming, reuse, patterns, and so on; finally, full management support in the areas of controllership is necessary. If these are in place, a business can become truly agile."

"How would you relate the necessary conditions of agility to achieving actual agile behavior?"

"There are, broadly speaking, two drivers of change. One is innovation, the introduction of something new; two, the need to react to something that occurred. The first is a proactive strategy; the second is a reactive necessity. Let us assume that your company is agile-mature. Now let us suppose there is a need to change an exist-

---

[61]MDA is sponsored by the Object Management Group, and allows for the specification of platform-independent models (PIMs) that may be subsequently translated into platform-specific models (PSMs) using various techniques and tools.

ing business process. Let us see if you can work through the scenario. Who wants to take a shot?"

After some hesitation, a black belt raised her hand. "I would assume that a repository of well-defined processes would exist," she began. "The PIQ team would search for the relevant process or processes that may be affected by the change. The team would use simulation and other analytical techniques to make changes to this process. Since it is all captured in one common model, the business analysts can hit the ground running and very quickly understand how the systems data would change. Am I on the right track?"

"Perfect," Jeff assured her. "Then what happens?"

A technical architect picked up the thread. "The business analyst would use the BPM platform to add more detail about the changes. The technical team would push the button to produce the BPEL and WSDL specifications. We would easily write the code or hook up the adapters to existing systems using the XML-based specs."

"Excellent. The BPM platform may also have a process engine that will execute the process directly, with very little code to be written, though that may be an idealized scenario."

A senior tester suggested, "Under SOA, testing would be minimized too, since it is easier to localize functionality to specific services. Enormous amounts of regression testing would be eliminated."

"How is that good?" asked another tester. "We'd lose our jobs!"

The room shook with laughter.

"Don't worry, we'll retrain you to spot errors and defects in process models," consoled a black belt.

"Let us not lose that important point brought up by this tester," advised Jeff. "Agility means doings things quickly and more efficiently. This frees up time for everyone, not just the QA team. A positive way to look at it is that it builds capacity within the company, allowing it to grow aggressively without adding cost. Your jobs would be more fun, more fulfilling, and more secure than ever."

"And we get paid too! Surely, that's an embarrassment of riches!" said a senior programmer.

"Speak of gravy on top!" quipped Jeff. "Now let us examine the second scenario, where we need to react to some trigger. What would be the most important prerequisite to a reaction?"

Various suggestions floated about the room:

"A policy covering the correct response to each situation."

"Training of employees."

"An agile systems architecture that allows quick response."

"Empowering employees to take action."

"Effective communication."

"A corporate culture that rewards initiative."

Jeff heard variations and elaborations of the above ideas. He shook his head when the buzz died down.

"All the things you mentioned are important," he said. "But the necessary condition for a reactive step to occur is the detection of the change event. Without knowing what occurred, or where it occurred, to whom it occurred, or what processes it impacts, it would not be possible to do anything about it. That is why, a very important capability of process management is BAM, or Business Activity Monitoring."

"Six Sigma covers this capability. It is called *Measure*, the 'M' of the DMAIC methodology," suggested a black belt.

"Not exactly," countered Jeff. "The *measure* phase of DMAIC deals with an analytical situation, not a transactional situation. The *control* phase of DMAIC does deal with transactional processes, but Six Sigma itself does not care *how* the process control happens. This is not a ding against Six Sigma, because Six Sigma's charter is not with the *how*, but with the *what*. BPM fills this gap by giving us BAM, which deals with the monitoring of transactions, most often in real-time."

"Sort of like using interest rate trends to guide investment policy versus using the interest rate of the day to price loans."

"Good analogy. The consumers of data used in the *measure* phase of Six Sigma projects are the PIQ folks and functional analysts. The primary consumers of data reported by a business activity monitoring solution are the operations managers. The data from the *measure* phase is used to improve the processes. The *control* phase establishes the control points and the tolerances. BAM helps you manage the processes."

"So, if we implement BAM as part of a process management solution, we are able to detect change events quickly. Where does the ability to react quickly come from?" another black belt wanted to know.

Jeff pointed to the black belt who had started off the prior scenario by alluding to a repository of processes.

"We just heard how a process repository facilitates knowledge management and analysis. Before we jump into agility, let us revisit one of the important pieces of information that should be attached to processes, namely, control points. Each of you have a different perspective on controls. The PIQ team knows how to define defects and specify tolerances on processes. They also measure cycle time, mean, variance, and yield of processes. If they are focused on a LEAN project, they also know how to identify and classify wasteful tasks. That is one group of control points. Let us call this group the *Six Sigma controls*."

A technical architect jumped in. "IT would be concerned about throughput of transactions, performance, response time from systems, availability of system resources, bottlenecks, and so on," she said. "Would these form another group of controls?"

"Correct. We should call them the *IT controls*. Any other control types, do you think?"

"I know senior management worries quite a bit about regulatory issues like Sarbanes-Oxley. I'm not sure if those could be classified as controls."

There was animated discussion on this topic. Most of the people in the room expressed their opinion that regulatory control points should be part of process management. Jeff concurred.

"Again, a good process management platform would allow you to specify *regulatory control* points. Sometimes, these controls points are no more than flags that say, 'Here be quicksand!' At other times, the control points could be detailed expressions of business rules that can be used by a Business Rules Engine to check for violations. Have we exhausted the types of control points."

There were assenting nods from the participants.

Jeff continued. "Well, there is in fact one more group of controls that management would care about. These are *internal audit controls*. Responsible executives monitor these even though there is no regulatory sword hanging over their heads. It just makes good business sense to do so. The best example of a framework that addresses various types of internal controls is called the COSO framework. It covers all kinds of enterprise risk, such as operational risk, credit risk, financial risk, and so on."

One analyst spoke up, looking for clarification. "So, we have four major groups of controls. What I am hearing is that each of us have the knowledge needed to define and specify one or more of these controls."

"Quite. As the process snake winds its way through the project, each of you can paint your own stripe on it. All of these control tags on the processes help the technology team either code or create dashboards to make the key metrics visible. Additionally, the IT team would know that some of the violations or exceptions call for notifications or escalations to be sent out to named people. So much for definition and detection of change events. The piece-de-resistance is the ability to change business processes quickly. When a change event occurs, the control point in question is tied to a process, a process step, or a group of process steps. An operations manager would be able to know exactly what, where, how, and to whom it happened. A really good BAM engine would even perform predictive analytics that can function as an early warning system."

A project manager interjected, "I think the dots are connecting for me. The operations manager would redeploy people or work to eliminate a bottleneck right away. They would know which transactions are aging past the pre-set limits. They'd know where inventory is running low. While this allows the managers to respond quickly, the underlying processes do not necessarily change. Am I reading this correctly?"

"So far so good," said Jeff, encouragingly. "The one final dot to connect is that agility means not only the ability of the business to respond quickly to change events, but also the ability to change its processes quickly. Process change happens in one of two ways: a business rule that is under the management of a business rules engine could change, in which case reprogramming by IT is not necessary, or process steps are eliminated or introduced, in which case some intervention by IT may be necessary."

"What goes around comes around!"

"Yes. I hope the above discussion highlighted the closed-loop nature of processes. It shows how feedback loops can be established by using the principles of process management, LEAN, and Six Sigma, all of them hooked up to a good BPM platform."

Jeff glanced at the glass doors. "I see Marty and Chuck are hovering outside. I think we have to conclude our discussion. I'd like to hear from you some of your takeaways."

"I think I understand now what you said about each of us having to pick up a new skill to make all this work," said one of the project managers.

"I'm very thrilled that with a change in our attitude towards processes, we can truly collaborate, share, and work as a team," offered a master black belt.

"I like how the process management concepts dovetail with the three laws of organizational synergy," said a black belt.

"I agree with all of the above," said another master black belt. "But I especially loved the idea of a process repository. This is something that I wondered about. I'm glad that BPM provides a real solution."

A developer spoke up. "I thought the conversion of process models into BPEL for execution in a process engine was the neatest idea. I'm going to go read up all about BPEL and WSDL."

Another project manager, looking at his notes, said, "I got a lot out of our discussion on control points and enterprise risk management. As a project manager, risk management is a challenge I appreciate. However, the controllership promoted by BPM goes beyond just project risks; it is a comprehensive view of process risk, project risk, and product risk."

"In addition to all of the above, I got to know a bunch of cute acronyms that I can impress my friends with," said another black belt.

Jeff made notes of these impressions from the employees.

"The takeaways that you all gleaned from our discussion are excellent and well-stated," he observed in closing. "I appreciate your enthusiasm and the fact that you came here with an open mind. Please continue to educate yourself about process management and closely related concepts such as service-oriented architecture, because your managers are very serious about implementing these ideas. For future reference, let us call this the 'United We Stand' meeting."

Key Points

- Sustaining the fundamental business model is the bare minimum that all employees must support completely, before thinking about innovation and growth.
- Both IT and Quality have different agendas in process improvement initiatives; however, these can be—and should be—complementary, and not antagonistic.
- A BPM platform should provide the right information about processes to the right parties.
- BPM's process repository fosters a common model and common understanding of the business.
- A good BPM platform eliminates trivialities and inefficiencies in analysis and design; in return, all parties in a project must acquire new skills and become disciplined in their modeling, analysis, and design activities.

15 From SOA to POA, From CIO to CPO

Jeff pulled into the expansive, gravel driveway of an imposing house in the upscale, nouveau-riche community of Barclay Estates. He vaulted out of his olive-green Mercedes CLK500 and strode up to the house. The crunch of the gravel under his feet sounded a pleasing, muted accompaniment. He stabbed at the door bell with a long, tapering forefinger. The lighted mother-of-pearl button, set to one side in an ornate mahogany panel, issued a deep musical chime that seemed to reverberate deep inside the bowels of the earth.

Jeff half-expected to be greeted by a uniformed English butler, but Barry himself opened the door. He led Jeff into a great room with vaulted ceilings. Tall windows were draped in heavy fabric that must have required at least two workmen to carry in. A red oak staircase curved out from one side, leading up to a huge loft area that would have comfortably housed a family of four. A plush rug in warm colors flowed down the middle of the stairs, fastened in place with gleaming brass rods. A cheerful log fire, set in an ornate white marble fireplace, burned brightly. The mansion exuded an air of subdued, rich elegance.

"Vodka on ice, club soda, slice of lime, right?" asked Barry, handing Jeff a crystal cut glass that sparked with the iridescence of the overhead chandelier.

"Shaken, not stirred, I see," observed Jeff. "Perfect!" He waited for Barry to join him.

"Prost!" said Barry, clinking his glass of Glenfiddich (two ounces of neat, 50-year old, single malt) lightly and carefully against Jeff's crystal. One is very careful with a family heirloom of specially commissioned Slovakian lead crystal.

"Cheers!" said Jeff, and took a sip of his vodka. He raised an eyebrow.

"Diaka," said Barry.

"Nothing but the best. I commend you. One hopes your excellent taste carries over to your selection of consultants as well."

"Full of p&v, aren't you? Glad you could join me today, Jeff." Barry led the way to a burgundy leather sofa accented in a maroon brocade. When they were seated, he pointed to a set of three plaques that stood upright on the coffee table. "Recognize them?" he asked Jeff.

They look like the three laws of organizational synergy," said Jeff, peering at them."

"Remnants of your famous *United We Stand* meeting. I heard very positive feedback from the IT and PIQ teams about it. It has been a long while since they've had excitement like that."

"You have an intellectually curious group of employees there, Barry. Count yourself lucky. In a few companies where I led similar discussions, I got a lukewarm reception. In those companies, the employees focused on all the reasons why BPM wouldn't work, and could they please get back to some boring ERP project."

"This certainly has been a very eye-opening journey for me. It will take time for all these ideas to jell together in my mind, but as long as I have someone who helps me and my team navigate these waters, I don't think I need to understand all this fully in order to benefit from it."

"I sense a proposition swinging by."

"Jeff, remember the sailing event? One of the things I explained to you was the importance of the role of a tactician. I'd like you to be our tactician and strategist. Are you open to it?"

"Very much. I appreciate your offer, Barry. I've had many deep discussions with you, your staff, and your employees. I think I am in a position to help you transform your company to a process-centric and process-mature company."

"Excellent. I'll have my folks set up the contract paperwork in the next few days."

They shook hands formally, and toasted each other.

"You can help me with one immediate need I have," said Barry. "Our company is expanding and we have a strong acquisition pipeline. I'm thinking of splitting our conglomerate into service and construction businesses. I'd like to build synergies in transaction processing. For starters, I'd like to hire a CIO and a PIQ Executive for one of the businesses. These two would complement Marty and Chuck for the other business. This time though, I'd like to get someone who understands process-centricity."

Jeff furrowed his brow in deep thought. "I have a suggestion," he said. "I think we have a golden opportunity here to look beyond a traditional CIO or PIQ role. I'd recommend that you look for a CPO, a Chief Process Officer."

Barry put his glass of scotch carefully on the side table, and leaned forward. He rested his right elbow on his knee, and cupped his chin with the palm of his right hand. "Interesting," he said. "Tell me more."

Jeff reciprocated the gesture, leaning forward. The flickering light of the fireplace highlighted his animated features.

"Marty and Chuck have been through a journey of discovery and learning of process management. They have been through the pain of having siloed teams trying unsuccessfully to collaborate. They realize that collaboration and synergy aren't simply a matter of attitude, intention, or willingness. They realize that certain processes that support the business processes—the *meta-processes*, if you will—must exist and be designed to make cooperation natural, and not a painful, psychological overhaul. Why not leverage that understanding they have gained, and let them both graduate into the role of CPO, one for each business?"

"I hadn't thought of that," said Barry. As was his practice when an idea fired his imagination, he got up and started pacing back and forth. "I suppose each of them has to learn a little bit about the other's function. I can see Marty absorbing PIQ, but wouldn't it be a stretch for Chuck to handle technical issues?"

"You may be underestimating the subject of process improvement and quality. I'm sure Marty will be able to pick it up, but it is no easier than Chuck picking up IT. In any case, Chuck doesn't need a thorough understanding of technical issues, any more than Marty needs to know how to test for normality of data. Chuck can hire an enterprise architect with deep experience in all things technical."

"I like this idea a lot. I propose a toast," said Barry, stopping to pick up his glass.

"Now," asked Barry, after they'd taken a generous sip of their libations. "How would you define the role and responsibilities of a CPO?"

"I have a few thoughts on that subject."

"Why doesn't that surprise me?"

"I'd propose that you break up each of your businesses into two types of sub-businesses. One part would continue to execute the daily operations, the management of transactions, the manufacturing, and so on. The other part would be a new entity that would become a Center of Competence. The Center would be your bridge from strategy to execution. It would be the company's way to make innovation happen. The Center of Competence would be the brain trust of the corporation. It would house and maintain the process knowledge, business models, best practices, analytics, and so on."

"I'm not really in favor of such an entity. In my experience, it would simply turn into a think-tank that slowly loses touch with the practicalities of business. The employees of the Center of Competence lose their transaction skills. They get disenchanted. Meanwhile, the operations people think the folks in this Center of Competence have nothing to do, but just sit around and think beautiful thoughts. Morale suffers all around."

"Don't I know it!" responded Jeff with feeling, recalling his own experience. "One solution is to make the Center of Competence a rotational posting, sort of a corporate sabbatical. A small number of employees could serve on it for a short period, say, three months, with overlap between them. They would work on improving processes, documenting their knowledge, take on special projects, pick up new skills, get re-trained, and so on. I recommend that your senior managers take turns at the Center of Competence for a longer duration, perhaps a year. After their stint, they would go back to their regular jobs energized and with a new appreciation for the business."

"It might work," said Barry, scratching his chin as he continued to pace. "By making it a rotational job, we make sure the Center doesn't become a stagnant, elitist club."

"Yes. So, in principle, does this idea resonate with you?"

"My gut tells me, *Yes*. How can we encapsulate this thought about the Center of Competence? Seems to me it has to be a law of organizational synergy."

"I agree. Its primary function is to give expression to the company's priorities, in a way that can be operationalized. So, I propose what I call the Zeroeth Law of Organizational Synergy, because this must precede the First Law."

Jeff grabbed a pen and a notepad from a side table, and wrote on it. When he was done, he gave it to Barry. On the notepad was written:

The Zeroeth Law

Management shall formulate corporate strategy and goals that maximize the value proposition of the corporation to its employees, customers, and society; management shall communicate this strategy and goals very clearly to the employees.

Barry said, "Well put." He picked up the plaque that captured the First Law and looked at it for a moment. "It seems to me that we now lost the symmetry in the laws."

"I'm addressing that, Barry," replied Jeff from across the room, where he was busily writing on another sheet of paper. When he was done, he came back and showed Barry the modified First Law:

The First Law

Employees shall be diligent and focused in the performance of their primary job tasks, except when this conflicts with the Zeroeth Law.

Barry digested this for a few moments. "This modified version of the First Law seems to give my employees a carte-blanche to stop working on anything that doesn't support the corporate strategy and goals. Is that wise?"

"This is an extension of the concept of jidoka. Remember that in the LEAN methodology, an assembly line worker is empowered to stop the line if he or she detects a fault. The same empowerment should be given to your employees regardless of their function, role, or position. The modified First Law is telling your employees not to perform their jobs mindlessly just because it is in their job description; instead, they should keep the big picture in mind. You may be pleasantly surprised how responsibly your employees will behave."

"Now that you put it like that, I agree with you. In general, my employees behave rationally. This type of empowerment can only instill more ownership and pride of workmanship in them. The only nagging doubt that I have about the Center of Competence concerns IT. I worry about shortchanging IT. That is too important a function to sideline."

"It warms my heart to hear you say that. As we discussed before, your IT department already understands the far-reaching implications of a service-oriented architecture. Under the guidance of a Chief Process Officer who heads up a Center of Competence, the service-oriented architecture should mature into a process-oriented architecture."

"SOA to POA?"

"We might as well call it that, since we are on a roll here."

Barry proposed a toast to POA.

Jeff picked up the thread after they refilled their glasses. "We started to talk about the role and responsibilities of the CPO," he said. "The CPO would head up the Center of Competence and operationalize the four laws of organizational synergy. The CPO would implement a process management platform, and expand the skills of the Quality people to take full advantage of BPM capabilities. Finally, the CPO would transform IT from a purely technical focus into an IT department that is completely aligned with the business, again by taking full advantage of BPM and SOA capabilities. This would be accomplished by building a Process-Oriented Architecture. I believe this would be a workable way to eliminate the dreaded business-IT divide."

"These are far-reaching and revolutionary changes," responded Barry. "I'd like to call an extra-ordinary meeting of our Board of Directors to propose this and get their reaction to it. I'd like to make it a two part agenda. In part one, I'd like to cover our state of business and go through the growth ideas we have on the table. In part two, I'd like to package up everything we discussed and have you make the presentation to the Board. You'll have to nail down a lot of details before then, such as your recommendations for operating mechanisms, ideal staffing of the Center of Competence, job descriptions, estimated costs, and so on. I'll ask Marty and Chuck to work with you on this."

"I'd be happy to lead this."

"Between now and then, we should think very hard about the real dineros, the real benefits, for the company. I want to make these benefits very real and very hard-hitting for the Board. You should include the numbers you threw about when you lectured us on innovation. To help us all as we expend some serious brain-cycles on the benefits, can you come up with a wire frame where we can hang our ideas?"

Jeff moved to the sideboard once more to sketch on the notepad. He spoke as he made notes.

"There is a cute graphic—what you so poetically called a wire frame—that I employ to help me think through this challenging topic. It is not the full solution obviously, and I know you are not looking for that right now. But it is a convenient device.

"I think of two distinct types of activities that we perform. The first is what I call the definitional activity, where we try to define a strategy, a growth idea, a process, or a specification for an enhancement. The second is what I call the execution, where we implement the defined strategy, idea, process, or specification. For both these types of activities, we can either perform them quickly and efficiently, or not. This gives us a 4-cell capability matrix that looks like this picture."

Here, Jeff presented his matrix to Barry:

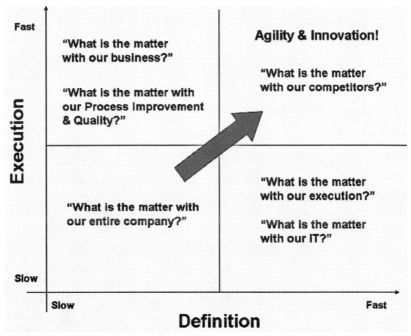

"The idea is to move from the lower left cell to the top right cell," explained Jeff. "Without a thoughtful program of process management, without the role of a CPO, and the rest of the ideas we talked about, there is a danger of moving your company to one of the other cells and getting stuck there. Clearly the other cells are not globally optimal solutions."

"Let us make use of this matrix to put some real numbers into these cells. Jeff, if you can come up with a starter list of some metrics and their definitions as they apply to each of the four cells, we can discuss at our next staff meeting. My team will carry that ball forward by providing some hard data."

"You can use that hard data to assess where you stand today with respect to this matrix."

"That's right. Then we make a business case for moving into the top right cell, where we clearly are not situated right now but ought to be. This whole exercise will take our discussion with the Board to a level that is definable, measurable, and actionable. Otherwise, we could just get bogged down in high-level, warm-and-fuzzy talks."

"Your company will gain immense competitive and sustainable advantage if you put this into practice," observed Jeff. He finished his drink and stood up. "I have to drive home now, so I'd better conclude with a sobering thought. One may get the impression that process management will solve all problems, including but not limited to world hunger. Well-managed processes are indeed a powerful, unifying force. However, they cannot be effective in a vacuum. The methodology and technology of process management are just two critical ingredients. Organizational culture and synergy are even more important."

"I completely agree," said Barry, warmly pumping Jeff's hand. He walked Jeff to the door, summarizing as he went. "Our growth is stalling because we don't institutionalize innovation. Like Alice in Wonderland, we run fast and furious but we seem to get nowhere. We work hard, but our return on time, the ROT, is pathetic. We go on a hiring binge hoping that throwing people at problems will somehow solve them. We waste enormous amounts of money on long-term ERP projects that yield no real benefits. We go into a panic or a catatonic stupor when faced with regulatory demands."

Barry opened the door, and Jeff stepped out. Outside, it had turned bitterly cold. Leaves that were warm with vibrant colors in the daylight turned into an amorphous gray in the dwindling twilight. Jeff turned around for a parting handshake. He stood framed in the baroque door way, the wind fluffing his great coat. The gentle lighting from the entrance hall played upon his angular features.

Barry reached out for a parting handshake, his strong grip promising trust and the start of an adventure. "I am thrilled that we have available to us a realistic weapon that we can use to make innovation, agility, controllership, and productivity real and achievable. Jeff, you introduced us to energizing ideas. Who'd have thought that processes have so much power!"

Key Points

- The time for the role of a Chief Process Officer (CPO) has come; given that IT has visibility into all the business functions, CIOs are uniquely placed to morph into CPOs.
- Once a company arrives at a high level of process maturity, it can benefit from a Center of Competence to house the brain trust of the corporation and to institutionalize process innovation.
- Frequent and consistent communication of corporate strategy by senior management to its employees is vital.
- Employees should feel empowered to question and improve processes; such empowerment fosters a sense of ownership and pride.
- A high level of maturity in both definitional and execution processes leads to continued innovation and agility.
- A fully mature process management capability that includes sophisticated technology coupled with a supportive organizational culture gives a company tremendous competitive advantage.

Glossary

AAGR:	Average Annual Growth Rate
BAM:	Business Activity Monitoring
BPE:	Business Process Engine
BPEL:	Business Process Execution Language
BPM:	Business Process Management
BPMN:	Business Process Modeling Notation
BPMS:	Business Process Management System
BRE:	Business Rules Engine
CAGR:	Compound Annual Growth Rate
CEO:	Chief Executive Officer
CFO:	Chief Financial Officer
CIO:	Chief Information Officer
COO:	Chief Operating Officer
CPO:	Chief Process Officer
CM:	Contribution Margin
CXO:	Chief *something* Officer
DMAIC:	Define, Measure, Analyze, Improve, Control
DFSS:	Design For Six Sigma
FASB:	Financial Accounting Standards Board
GAAP:	Generally Accepted Accounting Principles
IT:	Information Technology
MACRS:	Modified Accelerated Cost Recovery System
MDA:	Model-Driven Architecture
PIQ:	Process Improvement and Quality
POA:	Process-Oriented Architecture
ROA:	Return on Assets
ROE:	Return on Equity
ROI:	Return on Investment
ROT:	Return on Time
SDLC:	Systems Development Life Cycle
SOA:	Service-Oriented Architecture
SOX:	Sarbanes-Oxley
TLA:	Three-Letter Acronym
XML:	eXtensible Markup Language

Appendix: Dr. Sterllings' Laws

On Six Sigma (chapter 4)
Theorem: *BPM synergistically complements Six Sigma.*
Corollary: *Six Sigma Experts will NOT be out of a job.*

On the Conservation of Cost of Information (chapter 5)
Theorem: *The cost of collecting and recording information is constant in any given context, but the consequences of not collecting and analyzing it multiply the longer it is delayed.*
Corollary: *Make your process documentation as information-rich as you can, as early as you can, and you shall be freed from an impoverished analysis.*

On the Ecosystem of BPM (chapter 7)
$Future\_State = Current\_State * (SOA^{BPM} + BAM * BPM)$

On Slimming (LEAN) (chapter 11)
Theorem: *LEAN takes the fat out of processes. BPM keeps it out.*
Corollary: *Without BPM, lean processes crawl back to corpulence.*

On Compliance (chapter 13)
Theorem: *Process Management offers a disciplined, sustainable meta-process for controllership and compliance.*
Corollary: *If whips and chains ain't your thing, Come give BPM a fling.*

On Organizational Synergy (chapters 14 & 15)
The Zeroeth Law: *Management shall formulate corporate strategy and goals that maximize the value proposition of the corporation to its employees, customers, and society; management shall communicate this strategy and goals very clearly to the employees.*
The First Law: *Employees shall be diligent and focused in the performance of their primary job tasks, except when this conflicts with the Zeroeth Law.*
The Second Law: *Employees shall innovate and improve processes, except when this conflicts with the First Law.*
The Third Law: *Employees shall perform their tasks in a way that provides efficiencies to their colleagues, unless such performance conflicts with the First or Second Law.*

Index

Business Process Management: The Third Wave
The landmark book on BPM!